THE WEALTH-BUILDING BARBER

The 7 Keys for Building Wealth

Leronzo Williams

Disclaimer

Table of Contents

INTRODUCTION

From Clippers to Riches - My Journey to Financial Empowerment

"The way to get started is to quit talking and begin doing."

- Walt Disney

The Humble Beginnings

A leased booth and some clippers were the humble beginnings. I had no clients and no plan when I first started out; all I had was a burning desire to succeed and the faintest hint that my wild ambition could pay off. I would sit in that chair for what felt like hours on end, praying for a customer who would just stroll in. There was no more time to fill my pockets than there was in my appointment book. This might not be something I'm cut out for, I thought to myself. Perhaps this wasn't my calling all along.

You know, ever since I was a little kid, I thought of the neighborhood barbershop as the beating heart of our town. That's where all the guys would congregate, tell tales, and get their hair trimmed. When I was a little kid, I couldn't get enough of seeing the barbers cut long, unruly hair into neat, stylish designs. From a young age, I desired to be a part of the level of respect and camaraderie that I appreciated. Consequently, I enrolled in a barbering school, honed my skills, and saved up enough to rent a booth in a tiny downtown establishment.

But the reality of being a young, inexperienced barber with minimal clientele was far worse than I had imagined. The streets were calling my name, promising fast money and easy gains, and I got to be honest, there were times when that thought started to sound pretty enticing. I had witnessed too many individuals I grew up with going down that path, and they never came back. But when you're gazing at an empty booth with unpaid bills, the prospect of giving up and going back to that life seems almost too easy.

Discovering the Power of Financial Literacy

Something deep within me refused to quit still in it all. I wasn't ready to let go of this dream, not yet. That's when I had to make a decision - was I going to sink, or was I going to swim? I started looking at this game differently. It wasn't enough to just know how to cut hair - I had to learn how to operate a genuine business before I got run out of business. So, I started learning, reading, and watching everybody I could who was winning. I devoured literature on marketing, customer service, and financial management. I even started following some of the more successful barbers, picking their brains about the tactics that had made them prosper.

That's when I stumbled into something that would change everything - financial literacy. It was as if someone had flicked a switch in my brain. I didn't only need to make money; I needed to understand how to keep it and how to grow it. So, I started small. I saved every dollar I could. While all the other fellas were spending their salaries on the latest fashion or the newest gadgets, I was stashing and stacking, making sure every piece of money that came in was working for me. It wasn't easy, but I stayed disciplined. And you know what? That small bit of savings grew, and one day, it became enough to open up my very own barbershop.

Transforming a Dream into a Business

Opening the shop was one of the proudest moments of my life, but I didn't stop there. The shop was more than just a source of income, it was a symbol of resilience and possibility. I began to think beyond the daily grind of cutting hair. Each customer that walked in was an opportunity, not just for immediate earnings but for building relationships, trust, and repeat business. The walls of that shop became a canvas where I painted my dreams of a stable, prosperous future.

Running the barbershop required more than just technical skill with clippers. I had to master customer service, manage inventory, and ensure the environment was welcoming. One of my first big changes was improving the shop's appearance. A fresh coat of paint, comfortable chairs, and new mirrors transformed the space, giving it a modern yet cozy feel. Customers noticed, and they started bringing their friends and family. Business began to pick up, slowly but surely.

But as the business grew, so did my hunger for knowledge. I found myself asking questions like, "What's next?" and "How do I make this sustainable?" The idea of being a barber for the rest of my life was daunting. It wasn't because I didn't love the craft, I did, I really did. But I wanted more. I wanted to create something that could thrive even when I wasn't behind the chair.

Expanding the Vision

With the barbershop gaining traction, I started to explore additional income streams. That's when I decided to open a small hair supplies store adjacent to the shop. It wasn't a massive operation, but it catered directly to my existing customers. People could now leave with their favorite grooming products in hand, saving them a trip elsewhere. This not only increased my revenue but also solidified my shop as a one-stop destination for grooming and self-care needs.

I also began building relationships with other local businesses. Collaboration became a key strategy. For instance, I partnered with a nearby clothing store to host joint promotions. Customers who got a haircut at my shop would receive a discount at the clothing store and vice versa. These partnerships not only boosted sales but also fostered a sense of community among local entrepreneurs.

The Spark of Long-Term Thinking

As my confidence grew, so did my aspirations. I started asking myself, "What's my exit strategy? How do I ensure this isn't just a job but a lasting legacy?" That's when I began exploring retirement planning and investments. One of the first steps I took was opening a Roth IRA. Every week, I set aside $100, believing that small, consistent contributions would add up over time. For three years, I invested diligently, excited about the future I was building.

But life has a way of throwing curveballs. One day, I checked my Roth IRA balance and was shocked to see how little it had grown. Despite contributing over $16,000, my account balance barely exceeded $5,800. It was a wake-up call. I realized that relying solely on others to manage my money wasn't enough, I needed to take an active role in understanding and directing my investments.

This moment of realization didn't discourage me; it motivated me. I began reading about different investment vehicles, from mutual funds to real estate. The world of finance, once intimidating, started to feel like a game I could learn to play and win.

Leveling Up with Stocks and Investments

One day, when I was cutting a client's hair, he asked me whether I was in the stock market. At the time, I was experimenting a little bit, but I truly didn't grasp the game.

He informed me I was probably paying way too much for the stocks I owned and that I needed to start investigating the companies before I got in. That was another one of those turning-point moments. He started emailing me all these videos and tutorials, and I dug in, educating myself. I learned about concepts like buying the dip, waiting for equities to drop to a discount, and how to truly make the market work in my favor.

Initially, the stock market felt like a foreign language, with terms and strategies I could barely wrap my head around. But the more I learned, the more the pieces began to fall into place. Investing wasn't just about luck or picking trendy stocks; it was about understanding the fundamentals, reading financial statements, and spotting undervalued opportunities. I began treating every dollar as a soldier, sending it into battle with the mission of bringing back reinforcements.

Soon, I developed a portfolio that balanced risk and reward, combining blue-chip stocks with smaller, high-growth companies. Every successful investment boosted my confidence, and even my mistakes became invaluable lessons. The stock market, much like barbering, required patience, precision, and the ability to adapt to changing circumstances.

Building Generational Wealth

As I learned more, I began to realize that wealth wasn't just about accumulating money—it was about creating a legacy. I didn't want to simply grow rich; I wanted to establish a foundation for my family and my community. This mindset shift inspired me to diversify further, venturing into mutual funds, dividend-paying stocks, and ETFs. I discovered the power of compound interest, watching my earnings grow exponentially over time.

At the same time, I started sharing my journey with others. Friends, clients, and even fellow barbers began asking for advice. I'd find myself breaking down investment strategies during haircut appointments, turning the barbershop into an impromptu financial literacy classroom. It was rewarding to see others light up with the realization that they, too, could build wealth with the right knowledge and discipline.

The Choice of Your Next Move is Yours

Looking back now, from that struggling young barber renting a booth and ready to give up, to becoming a barbershop owner, a property owner, and an investor, I see it all so clearly. This quest wasn't just about cutting hair; it was about cutting through the limits that were keeping me back. Financial knowledge was the key that unlocked the door to my future.

For so long, I had been conditioned to assume that success meant having a conventional 9-to-5 job, maybe starting a small business on the side, and, if I was really lucky, retiring with a modest pension. But as I educated myself on economics, investing, and wealth-building tactics, my entire outlook changed. I recognized that the way to true financial freedom and generational wealth was right in front of me, if only I had the confidence to grasp it.

It hasn't been an easy route, and there have been plenty of failures and hurdles along the way. But with each challenge I've overcome, I've developed a greater grasp of how to navigate the complex financial world and make my money work for me rather than the other way around. And now, I'm on a mission to share what I've learned with my fellow barbers and beyond, because I know that the tools for earning wealth are accessible to all of us, we just have to be ready to put in the work.

Lessons in Discipline and Growth

The significance of self-control was driven home to me on the road to financial independence. When I first started my barbershop, I was very careful with my money. I reinvest in my business while others spent on pleasures. For instance, I immediately attracted more customers after upgrading equipment and establishing a friendly atmosphere. I was able to increase my income and lay the groundwork for future growth into related businesses by employing this reinvestment technique.

In my early years, I chose to invest some of my revenue on marketing. To draw in more consumers, I made loyalty cards, gave discounts for word-of-mouth, and even held community activities. These endeavours did not produce instant gratification, but they bore fruit in the form of a continual stream of devoted customers who ensured that my chairs were always filled.

This is where the true journey begins, my friend. Will you stay stuck in that chair, or will you rise up and improve your life? The option is yours, but I'm telling you - the tools are right here in your hands. All it takes is the bravery to trust in yourself and the discipline to start putting the ideas of financial literacy into practice.

So, what do you say? Are you ready to become the Wealth Building Barber?

Case Study: John's story

Take John, a barber battling with debt and intermittent revenue. By attending financial literacy classes and creating a budgeting system, he improved his finances. John devoted 20% of his weekly salary to savings and investing. Within three years, he had saved enough to operate his own barbershop, earning both financial stability and freedom. John's path is proof that with the appropriate mindset and tools, anyone can change their situation around.

CHAPTER 1

The 1% Mindset That Explains Why Most Barbers Stay Broke

"Do not go where the path may lead, go instead where there is no path and leave a trail." —Ralph Waldo Emerson

It is entirely possible for you to make a lot of money and pull in millions from the multibillion-dollar barbering industry. But let's talk about the facts: 95% of barbers are broke when they retire. There are no assets, no retirement plans, and no investments to speak of. Only faded hopes and worn-out clippers. Only 4% reach six figures, and just 1% become millionaires. Why? Because they understand it. They realize something most barbers do not: the importance of financial literacy. They understand how to convert the constant stream of revenue from behind their chair into an ocean of wealth.

From infancy to the tomb, a man requires a haircut and shave. That is why the game is recession-proof. Regardless of what is going on in the world, the need for grooming persists. However, our success in this game will be determined by three factors: the importance of what we do, our ability to execute it well, and the difficulty of replacing us. But here's the problem, most of us concentrate solely on the skill. We believe we have mastered the fuzzy fade, taper, and ultra-crispy edge-up. The truth, however, is that skill accounts for only 10% of the game. What about the remaining 90 percent? That is straight business.

Business is where wealth is created. The question is not, "Can you cut?" The question is, can you build? How do you transform those hands that move with precision with each cut into instruments of financial freedom? How can you attract leads, convert them into loyal clients, and generate a consistent stream of revenue that not only pays the bills but also grows an empire? Let us break it down. Assume you cut 40 heads every week at $50 per cut. That's $2,000 every week. Multiply it by 52 weeks, and you're looking at

$104,000 every year. Congratulations, you've just reached six figures. That's a good start, but what if you make a few adjustments? What if you raise your rates or volume? Cut 60 heads every week for $50 each, and you'll make $156,000 per year. Alternatively, raise your price to $60 for each cut and retain the headcount at 50 - that's $156,000 per year.

But why stop there? What if you add services like facials, before-hours, or after-hours cuts to increase your value while raising the entire price? You're now adding additional money to your account. Don't forget about brushes, wave caps, shampoos, and beard oils - all of the goods your customers already use but purchase elsewhere that you may sell. Why not become their one-stop shop? You are no longer just a barber; you are a business that provides barbering services. When you start stacking streams of income like this, it becomes quite easy to accumulate wealth. However, most barbers make a mistake here: the money comes in quickly and leaves just as quickly. Without a strategy or a plan, $100,000 might disappear before you know it. Consider this; what if you lived below your means for three to five years? What if you took 50% of your wages and invested the remainder? That's how you progress from producing money to creating wealth. You're not just cutting hair, you're establishing a legacy.

Think about it. If you invested in the stock market, you could have a portfolio that not only sustains your current lifestyle but also increases on its own. The stock market has historically returned roughly 10% per year on average, which implies that if you invested $50,000 every year for ten years, you would have more than $700,000 in your portfolio, even after accounting for market fluctuations. This is the power of compound growth and sustained investment. What if you invested in real estate? By buying investment properties and renting them out, you can generate a consistent stream of passive income to augment your regular profits. Real estate has historically been a successful wealth-building tool, with an average yearly return on investment of 10-12%. And when the value of your homes increases over time, you may use that equity to buy new investment properties, resulting in a snowball effect.

Perhaps you decide to launch a new store or even a barber school. Diversifying your revenue streams allows you to construct numerous engines of wealth rather than relying solely on the chair. That is the game. That is how you join the 1%: you use your clientele's consistent stream of money to invest and grow its worth.

It begins with a vision. You must envision your ideal life and build a business to support it. Then, based on that vision, you create goals, establish plans to reach those goals, and take conscious action steps every day, and you will achieve the desired outcome. Without vision, you'll be like the 95%: stuck, broke, and wondering what went wrong.

Essential Investments

So, let's break down three essential investments you'll need to make as a wealth-building barber:

1. **Invest in Yourself.**

Who are you becoming? That is the true question requiring a moment of meditation to answer. Before you can accumulate wealth, you must first acquire a wealth of knowledge. You may have the sharpest clippers and the freshest cuts, but if your mind isn't keen, inventive, and resourceful enough to absorb the proper information, take strategic action, and make sound investments, you're in trouble.

Success is an internal job. You cannot simply stumble into riches; you must become the type of person capable of maintaining it. Your foundation consists of mindset, knowledge, and discipline. Investing in yourself is the first step in living a free life and leaving a lasting legacy. Develop the habits of a winner. Improve your thinking. Develop the mental and emotional power required to rise above.

For me, my desire for progress drove me to read book after book, listen to hours of audio, attend conferences and workshops, and participate in mentoring programs. What you focus on determines who you become. Exposure leads to expansion. If you put greatness inside, you will only get greatness out. According to B.B. King, "The beautiful thing about learning is that no one can take it from you."

When was the last time you engaged in your personal development and skills outside of the chair? Most people never invest in themselves; they work for money but never use it to benefit their future selves. They remain in survival mode, seeking the next cut rather than focusing on the person they must become to advance.

2. **Invest in Your Higher Power.**

No journey to wealth is complete without a purpose. True wealth is more than just dollar signs and bank balances; it is based on purpose. Without a larger mission to anchor you, all the money in the world will not provide long-term fulfillment. It would be beneficial if you had something bigger than yourself to propel your hustle, something that adds depth and direction to your work. Whether it's faith, spirituality, or a deeply personal sense of mission, this higher power will keep you going when times are tough.

When you integrate your career with a higher calling, every dollar made becomes more valuable, and every accomplishment becomes more significant. This deeper connection keeps you grounded while you navigate the highs and lows of wealth accumulation. Money may inspire you, but purpose will fuel your resilience, allowing you to stay focused when things go rough. A higher power sharpens your vision, fortifies your character, and assures that the legacy you leave is one of both financial success and long-term effects.

Investing in this stage of your journey means more than just keeping afloat; it means creating something that will withstand the test of time. Because wealth, when driven by purpose, transforms from transient prosperity to something transformative and lasting.

3. **Invest in Your Future.**

This is the stage at which you put your creation to use. Stocks, real estate, and other companies generate revenue streams that continue even while you are not working.

The barber game is about more than just the fade; it is about the future. The question is, will you join the 1% who actually comprehend this? Or will you fade away like the others, wondering what could or should have been?

Let's take a look at some particular strategies to invest in your future.

- **Stocks and Investing:** As previously said, the stock market is an effective wealth-building strategy. By continuously investing a percentage of your income, you can leverage compound growth to accumulate a significant portfolio over time. Index funds and ETFs are excellent places to start since they give broad market exposure while minimizing risk.

- **Real estate investments:** Real estate investments can generate a consistent stream of passive income while also increasing equity and value over time. You can build wealth without exchanging your time for dollars by leveraging other people's money (via mortgages) and efforts (via property management).

- **Business ventures:** Opening additional barbershop locations or even establishing a barber training school might help you diversify your income and generate new cash streams. These business enterprises can generate both active and passive income, accelerating your wealth-building efforts.

- **Entrepreneurial Pursuits:** Your barbering talents and experience can be applied to various business ventures, such as producing barbering-related products and services or even franchising your own brand. The idea is to always explore new ways to apply your knowledge and expertise outside of the chair.

Your future is in your hands. It's time to sharpen your plan, step up your game, and carve your path to a life of prosperity and freedom, as well as legacy.

Moving from Survival to Significance

The distinction between the 95% who remain broke and the 1% who acquire wealth is not simply about statistics; it is about thinking. Most barbers have a survival attitude, focusing primarily on making ends meet and pursuing the next cut. However, the 1% think and act with a sense of significance.

The survival mindset states, "I need to make as much money as possible today to pay my bills." The significance mindset states, "I am creating something greater than myself that will have long-term value and impact."

The survival mindset is reactive, always extinguishing fires and chasing the next disaster. It's waking up every morning stressed about bills, hoping that enough clients show up to keep the lights on. The survivalist barber is constantly in hustle mode but never in control of their financial destiny. They work harder, not smarter, relying solely on their time and energy to make ends meet.

The significance mindset, on the other hand, is proactive. It's about preparing for the future, building systems, and investing in opportunities that ensure long-term stability and growth. A barber with this mindset doesn't just think about today's income but visualizes a financial map that leads to freedom. They focus on creating wealth streams that work for them even when they're not physically cutting hair.

As a barber who just works from the chair, your income is limited by the number of hours you can work each day. But imagine you start offering luxury services like beard treatments and facials, selling haircare goods, and even renting out your shop space to other barbers. You are no longer limited by your time; you have created a system that generates revenue from many sources.

When you transition from a survival attitude to a meaningful mindset, you stop viewing your work as only a job and instead see it as a wealth-building machine. You stop exchanging time for dollars and begin accumulating assets that work for you. You stop living paycheck to paycheck and begin living with meaning, intention, and legacy.

This shift often starts with asking a simple question: "What am I building?" If your goal is just to get by, you'll stay stuck in survival mode. But if your goal is to create something lasting, you'll naturally start making smarter decisions. Instead of spending $1,000 on the latest sneakers or gadgets, you'll think about how that money could grow through investments.

Case Study: John's story

Remember John from the introduction? When we last left him, he was figuring out how to accumulate wealth. After saving every penny, John founded his own barbershop and added value through premium services and retail merchandise. But John did not stop there. He accepted the significance mindset and started investing.

First, John invested a portion of his salary in index funds, letting compound growth work its magic. Then, to save money on housing, he acquired a duplex and rented one unit while living in another. Over time, the rental money from his home enabled him to expand his investments, purchasing more real estate and even considering franchising his barbershop brand. Ten years later, John is more than simply a barber; he's a mentor, community leader, and money maker. His path exemplifies the power of moving from survival to relevance.

Tools for the Transition

To advance beyond survival to relevance, you'll need to adopt the following tools:

1. **A vision board:** This allows you to clearly visualise your goals and the measures required to accomplish them.
2. **A budget:** Keep track of every dollar you spend to ensure that it is in line with your long-term goals.
3. **Investments:** Learn about stocks, real estate, and other ways to increase your money.
4. **Mentorship:** Surround yourself with people who are currently living the life you desire.

Creating Meaningful Impact

This is the 1% mindset. It's not just about cutting hair; it's about forging a route to financial independence, generational wealth, and a life of genuine importance. Consider this: your barbershop is more than just a place for haircuts; it's a source of inspiration for young barbers, clients leave with more than just a fresh cut, and you're known for making a positive impact in the community.

Are you prepared to join their ranks?

Summary of Key Takeaways

- The 1% mindset is about building wealth through strategic thinking, not just working harder.
- Transitioning from a survival mindset to a significance mindset requires planning, discipline, and a vision for the future.
- Creating multiple income streams and living below your means are essential steps to financial independence.
- Building a legacy is about more than making money; it's about creating lasting impact and generational wealth.

The transition from survival to significance is more than just a financial one; it's a personal adjustment. To break away from the cycle of living pay cheque to pay cheque, you must have the confidence and vision to understand what is possible when you adopt the "1% mindset." Every barber may achieve long-term success by using the correct equipment and focussing on continual progress. The choice is yours:

will you continue in the grind of survival, or will you rise to the level of significance?

Revision Questions

1. Why do you think most barbers focus primarily on perfecting their skills rather than understanding the business side of barbering?

    - Reflect on your own approach: Are you dedicating time to learning about marketing, customer retention, and financial management? Why or why not?

    - What strategies could you implement to start balancing skill mastery with business knowledge?

    - Imagine shifting your focus: How might that impact your long-term financial success?

____

____

2. Imagine you currently cut 40 clients per week at $50 per cut. How could you optimize your pricing, services, or weekly schedule to increase your yearly income?

    - If you raised your rates by $10, how much more could you earn annually?

- What premium services (e.g., grooming consultations or after-hours appointments) could you offer to justify higher pricing?
- How could you attract more clients without sacrificing quality or overworking yourself?

____

____

____

____

____

____

____

____

____

____

____

____

____

____

3. Living below your means is described as a wealth-building strategy. What sacrifices could you make today to achieve financial freedom faster?

    - List three expenses you could reduce or eliminate to increase your savings rate.
    - How would reinvesting those savings into assets like real estate or stocks improve your financial stability?
    - Imagine the long-term benefits of living frugally for five years. What would financial freedom look like for you?

____

____

____

____

____

____

____

____

____

____

____

____

____

____

4. The chapter emphasizes creating multiple income streams. How can you expand your barbershop into a multi-revenue business?

    - Could you sell grooming products, offer online courses, or partner with other businesses to diversify your income?

    - How would creating a subscription service for your clients, such as monthly grooming plans, affect your revenue?

    - What steps would you take to ensure each new income stream complements your existing services?

____

____

____

____

____

____

____

____

____

____

____

____

____

____

5. How does financial literacy empower barbers to move from surviving to thriving?

    - Reflect on the areas of financial literacy you currently lack. How can addressing these gaps transform your business?

- If you could learn one financial skill this month (e.g., budgeting, credit management, or investing), what would it be and why?

- Think about a financial mistake you've made in the past. How could better financial knowledge have helped you avoid it?

____

____

____

____

____

____

____

____

____

____

____

____

____

____

6. Building a legacy is about more than just making money. What steps can you take today to ensure your work leaves a lasting impact?

   - What would it mean to mentor younger barbers or start programs that teach financial literacy within your community?

   - How could creating a succession plan for your business or investing in long-term assets contribute to generational wealth?

   - Visualize your legacy 20 years from now. What does success look like for you, and how does it impact others?

____

____

____

____

CHAPTER 2

Cash vs. Credit (The Game of Wealth)

"Wealth consists not in having great possessions, but in having few wants." —Epictetus

The Myth That "Cash is King"

As master barbers, there is the need to understand how to make money. Our ability, work, and hustle all lead to cash in hand, a consistent stream of clients, and a thriving business. But here's the catch: cash isn't king. Yes, you've heard it before: "Cash is king, credit is trash." But let me tell you something that thinking keeps you small. We're playing chess, not checkers. In chess, the pawn is not the king. It's only a piece that helps you advance. The true power? That is represented by your assets and cash flow, often known as your Queens and Kings.

Growing up, I always felt the goal was to make the most money possible. Stack that cash, keep it safe, and you're set, right? Boy, was I mistaken? That's the poverty attitude, my friend. The wealthy do not think like that at all. They recognize that money is only the beginning; it is the raw material used to create actual prosperity.

Power of Assets and Cash Flow

In chess, the queen is the most powerful piece on the board. She goes in all directions, controls the battlefield, and prepares for victory. In your life, assets are the Queen. Those are your stocks, real estate, and business enterprises, which increase in value over time. These are the moves that result in generational wealth. They're not just making you money; they're also making you free by allowing you to reclaim your time and make better investments.

I recall when I first began to understand this concept. I was sitting in my barbershop calculating the day's cash when I had this insight. All of this money I was generating was amazing, but it wasn't helping me in the long run. It was just sitting there, gradually losing value to inflation. That's when I realized I needed to adjust my approach.

Avoiding Savings Trap

We do not save or hoard money. That is poor thinking. You're placing your money in a savings account, thinking it's safe. But guess what? That account pays you 0.003% interest. Do the math: it will take 2,400 years to quadruple your money! 2,400 years! Meanwhile, inflation depletes your wealth on a daily basis. Every money that sits still loses its worth. You believe you're saving, but you're actually losing. That is why the wealthy do not hoard money; instead, they distribute it, invest it, and watch it grow.

Now let me explain what I do. I don't have a traditional savings account; instead, I save in my S&P 500 account. Why? Because it gives me a 14% return. That is how you stay ahead of the game. The sole reason I keep cash is for two reasons: insurance against the unexpected and collecting funds for investment. You must safeguard yourself with an emergency fund, but after that, every dollar should be working for you by being invested in growing and multiplying assets.

Chess Analogy: Pawns, Queens, and Kings

Queens give birth to kings. When your assets are properly managed, they generate cash flow, which is the true king of wealth. Cash flow is more than simply money in the bank; it represents freedom. It's waking up knowing that your money is working for you while you're doing what you enjoy. But the trouble is that too many of us give up our Queens for Pawns. We keep that money, thinking we're playing it safe, while in reality, we're just playing a little.

So, would you sacrifice a queen for a pawn in chess? Hell no! You trade your Pawns (cash) for Queens (assets), which produce more Kings (cash flow). This is how the wealthy play. They move their cash through assets that generate additional cash flow, which generates more assets. It is a cycle and a system. It's another method to put money to work for you long after you've left your desk job.

Compound Interest Advantage

It's exactly like establishing a garden. If you want a crop, you should not eat the seeds. You plant them. You nourish them. Gradually, the tree bears fruit and each piece of fruit contains more seeds to plant. How can you hope to improve your future if you spend your money foolishly and live for today without thinking about tomorrow?

I'll never forget when I first invested $1,000 in an index fund. Watching it grow to $1,200 in a year may not sound dramatic, but it was a revelation. That $200 wasn't from cutting more hair or working longer hours, it came from my money working for me. Multiply that by 10 years, and you've got a roadmap to freedom.

We had to cease playing for the time being. Every dime you make behind the chair is a seed. However, money must be planted in long-term investments such as real estate, equities, and enterprises. This is about ensuring that the 40-year-old version of you appreciates the 20-year-old version for being wise, for foregoing the short-term joy for long-term freedom because you were disciplined. Small actions lead to large results, and every disciplined effort yields several benefits.

The Power of Small Moves.

Let's talk about the strength of little movements. A one-percent shift in your habits can transform your life. Do you read merely ten pages per day? That's 20 novels per year. Do you walk one mile every day? That's 365 miles each year. Do you only save $100 per week? That's $5,200 every year. Compound interest is real, and it is the key to creating money. Small, steady movements that add up over time. But it requires discipline.

The limits of cash

Now in the talk about money sure cash provides instant power. You can see, touch, and use it. You have complete control over it, and cash can save your life in an emergency. But what about cash alone? It is feeble. It's like the pawn in chess: valuable, yet restricted. If it is misplaced or stolen, it is gone forever. No protection. There's no backup. And what about holding onto cash? You are losing money every day due to inflation. The value of your money decreases the longer it lies motionless. That is why the wealthy do not simply hold cash; they shift it. They invest in it. They make it work and put it in circulation.

The Power of Credit

However, credit is a very different game. Credit is leverage. It's the instrument that will take you from hustling for every dollar to having money flow to you. With strong credit, you'll be able to borrow more money and pursue more opportunities. Whether it's purchasing a home, starting a business, or making decisions that money alone could never get you into. If you play your cards correctly, you will also receive protection, fraud protection, cash-back rewards, and months of interest-free money.

John's Journey into Credit Mastery

John's story provides a clear example. After stabilizing his barbershop income and putting systems in place, he started exploring the power of credit. One day, John read about leveraging 0% interest credit cards for wealth-building. Skeptical but curious, he decided to give it a try. He found a property valued at $18,000 but listed for $10,000 due to its condition. Using the credit card, he acquired the property, invested in minor renovations, and within three months, flipped it for a $20,000 sale. After repaying the credit card, John walked away with $8,000 in profit and still held an asset to generate further income. This experience showed him the potential of credit when used wisely, turning what seemed like debt into an opportunity for wealth creation.

With this success, John didn't stop. He started using credit strategically for his business, expanding into grooming products and leasing more chairs in his shop. Each step wasn't just about spending, it was about creating value and ensuring that every dollar borrowed came back with interest. John's story is a testament to the fact that credit isn't a burden; it's a tool that can elevate your hustle into an empire.

Stop Seeing Credit as Debt

Stop assuming that credit equals debt. Credit is a tool. And if you have a strong credit history, you may grow your empire in ways that cash cannot. You can get cash back, have your credit limit increased every few months, and use it to fund your aspirations. You are not simply borrowing money; you are setting yourself to play the game in the same way that the wealthy do.

So, cash or credit? It's not a matter of choosing one over the other; it's about understanding when to employ both. Cash currently provides you control, but what about credit? Credit provides you the ability to develop something larger than yourself. Something that will last. Something that provides freedom for you, your family, and your legacy.

Breaking the System's Chains

Let's be honest for a second. Did you know that the US currency is composed of 75% cotton? Think about it. With the wrong perspective, you're still picking cotton as a slave behind the chair. You may not be physically restrained, but you are in your head and wallet. Modern slavery is no longer physical; rather, it is mental and financial. If we don't grasp how money works, we're trapped in a system meant to keep us broke, hustling but never truly winning. Dressed up with a slew of worldly illusions, we become slaves to our surroundings, wants, and, most importantly, a system rather than conquering it.

The truth is that the game is stacked against us. The powers that be aim to keep us in our place, chasing paper and never moving forward. But, you know what? That's ridiculous. We're not following their rules anymore. We're going to learn the actual game, which the wealthy have been playing all along. And we want to use every tool at our disposal be it cash, credit, assets, and cash flow, to create the type of life and legacy that we deserve.

Remember, we are playing chess not checkers. Move your pawns wisely, protect your queens, and let your kings reign.

Summary of Key Takeaways

- Credit is leverage and can be a powerful tool when used responsibly to build wealth.
- John's story illustrates how credit can be used to create opportunities and generate cash flow.
- Balancing cash and credit strategically allows for greater financial freedom and long-term wealth creation.
- Breaking free from the mental chains of financial limitation requires understanding the game and using every tool available.

The real wealth game isn't just about working harder; it's about working smarter. Cash and credit are tools, and the way you use them determines whether you're playing to survive or to create a legacy. As John's journey shows, by thinking strategically and taking calculated risks, you can achieve financial independence and build a future that's larger than yourself.

Remember, every move you make can bring you closer to financial freedom, whether it's investing in an asset or leveraging credit. The key is to learn, adapt, and play the game with the mindset of a master strategist.

Revision Questions

1. Imagine you're running a barbershop with steady cash income. How could shifting your mindset to focus on assets and credit improve your financial situation?

- What challenges might arise if you continue to rely solely on cash?
- Can you identify one asset or investment opportunity you'd explore if you had access to credit?
- How could leveraging credit responsibly create new opportunities for your business?

____

____

2. Let's talk about compound interest. Have you ever thought about how saving $100 a month could grow over 10 years?

- What would happen if you invested that money in an account earning 10% annually? Try to picture the long-term growth.

- Can you think of one investment, like stocks or real estate, where compounding could significantly impact your wealth?
- How can starting small today help you build wealth for the future?

____

____

____

____

____

____

____

____

____

____

____

____

____

____

3. Picture this: You've just deposited $10,000 in a traditional savings account. What happens to its value over time if it earns minimal interest?

- What alternative options, like investing in index funds or real estate, could you explore to make that money grow?
- How can you strike a balance between maintaining an emergency fund and actively growing your wealth?
- Imagine setting up an investment plan today. How might that decision pay off 5 or 10 years down the road?

____

____

____

____

____

____

____

____

____

____

____

____

____

____

4. Think about credit as a tool. If you were given access to a 0% interest credit card, how would you use it to grow your wealth?

- Could you use it to fund a business idea, invest in real estate, or cover initial expenses for a profitable project?

- What steps would you take to ensure the debt is manageable and beneficial to your goals?

- Reflect on the potential rewards: How could credit elevate your financial position in ways cash alone cannot?

____

____

____

____

____

____

____

____

____

____

____

____

____

____

5. Let's discuss cash flow. Imagine your barbershop generates $5,000 a month in revenue but has $4,500 in expenses. How would you improve cash flow to create more breathing room?

- Could you increase revenue by adding services or products?

- How about reducing unnecessary expenses without compromising quality?

- What would it feel like to have consistent, positive cash flow creating stability for your business and personal life?

____

____

____

____

____

____

____

____

____

____

____

____

____

____

6. Discipline is the backbone of financial success. If you had to commit to one habit that could transform your finances, what would it be?

- Could it be cutting back on unnecessary spending, setting aside a fixed percentage of your income for investments, or educating yourself on financial strategies?
- How would those habits impact your financial journey over time?
- Reflect on John's journey: What specific actions did he take that you could apply to your own life? How would those choices transform your financial trajectory?

____

____

____

____

____

____

____

____

____

____

____

____

____

____

CHAPTER 3

Mastering Stock Investing for Barbers

"The stock market is designed to transfer money from the Active to the Patient." – Warren Buffett.

The Power of Passive Income

What I'm about to tell you, as I have rightly said, has the potential to alter not only your financial situation but also the legacy you leave to future generations. The time we put in at our desks is worthwhile, but we're wasting it if we just trade our hours for cash. You need to know how to put your money to work for you if you want to invest in the stock market because doing so can change your life.

Consider this: you work hard and get paid for just one haircut when you cut someone's hair. Suppose, however, that the same cut continues to reward you even after you have departed from the store that is the effect of stock market investments. Now that you're putting your money to work for you, you're no longer exchanging time for money. Having a team of employees who clock in and earn money even when you're not there is like having a Secret Santa. The secret to creating true, long-term wealth is passive income, and that is its power.

Imagine entering your barbershop one morning and being greeted by the usual hum of clippers and the aroma of freshly lathered aftershave. You look at your phone and see that you made an extra $500 overnight from your stock investments while you were asleep. You didn't have to take on more clients, work double shifts, or chop an extra head. That's why passive income is so great, even if you aren't using the clippers, you can still make money with it.

We are taught that perseverance is rewarded. But clever work is even more lucrative? The secret to achieving time freedom is passive income. The wealthiest barbers intentionally place their money where it grows on its own, rather than performing 16-hour stints in an attempt to maximize their daily earnings. They are the ones who are investing well so that they can retire to the chair as their fortune continues to grow.

The Dangers of Idle Cash

We've been told for far too long that saving money and keeping it is the secret to financial freedom. The fact is, though, that any money that isn't helping you is gradually perishing. The value of it is decreasing daily due to inflation. Do you have $100 today? Next year, it will be worth less. You are allowing it to deteriorate and disintegrate if you do not invest it.

Let's talk about these banks honestly now. You believe that your money is safe when you leave it in a savings account. The bank, meanwhile, is making major movements, turning that money, and offering you a meager 0.03% return. Consider this: your money is merely sitting there while the bank makes wealthy investments in stocks, real estate, and other endeavors. Why give them your money to play that game? It should be you who takes action and increases your riches. Investing in the stock market gives you authority. You're setting yourself up for success, not letting the bank win.

Look at the circumstance from a perspective where one of your pricey pair of clippers has merely been idle seating time away somewhere, will it still be worth that expense over time? Money is similar in that it has promise but loses value when left alone. Inflation is like rust eating away at your hard-earned money. If you only save and don't invest, your wealth is effectively withering away."

I learned the hard way. At one point, I was saving thousands of dollars every year, amassing wealth, and feeling accomplished, until I noticed I was losing money due to inflation. That represented a turning point for me. I took control, learned investing, and shifted my strategy from hoarding money to making it grow. What's the difference? Now, my money generates bigger revenue.

You need to change your perspective from considering yourself only a barber to considering yourself a wealth creator. How good are you at cutting hair? It is your art, your talent, and it has great power. Don't stop there, however. Put your money to work in the stock market by using it to buy securities. From surviving to thriving, that's how you change the narrative. I know barbers who put in a lot of labor. You must stand for long hours and ensure that your clients leave feeling rejuvenated. You can't chop your hair permanently, though. One day, your body will require a rest, or perhaps you'll wish to spend more time with your loved ones. When you're not behind the chair, will your money still contribute to your success? This is the distinction between earning a living and accumulating real riches.

Defining Your "Why"

Prior to investing in the stock market, you must clearly define your "why." What are you trying to achieve? Is the goal to someday retire and be able to live off of passive income? Do you wish to purchase real estate? Or are you attempting to create riches for future generations that will provide for your children and grandchildren? Stock market investment can help you achieve your objectives, but you must have a plan. Don't just follow the crowd and do what they're doing. Using someone else's tools without understanding how to use them is analogous to that. Knowing why you're making your moves is the first step toward understanding them.

Maintaining discipline and focus is considerably simpler when you have a clear idea of what you hope to accomplish. There may be ups and downs in the stock market, but it will be simpler to weather the storms if you know what you're aiming for. Imagine it as if you were cutting a customer's hair; every cut is guided by your precise vision of the finished look, and I t's the same with investing. To determine the best course of action to reach your destination, you must have a clear understanding of it.

The Importance of Research

Imagine attempting to cleanly fade someone without any prior expertise. You wouldn't, would you? Before you pick up the clippers, you should learn, practice, and perfect your technique. Investing is no different. Avoid buying stocks just because everyone is talking about them. Finish your homework. Research the businesses you plan to invest in. What are they doing? How do they generate revenue? Do they struggle or are they growing? Let's face it, no business is flawless. Similar to how every haircut might present difficulties, every stock carries hazards. Before investing your hard-earned money in any stock, you should be aware of its advantages and disadvantages. That's the difference between the gamblers and the true investors. You're not just throwing your money at the market and crossing your fingers when you do your homework. You're taking calculated risks, making well-informed choices, and making astute actions that will ultimately pay off.

It all comes down to knowing the basics. You cannot successfully invest if you do not understand the companies, the industries, and the market trends, just as you would not attempt to trim hair without knowing the fundamentals. You will be better able to handle the ups and downs and make wise investing choices the more knowledgeable you are.

Putting money into anything without first determining its style is like cutting someone's hair without consulting them. Obviously, you wouldn't act that way. Before beginning, you would carefully determine the client's hair type, style preferences, and the most effective procedure. Investing works the same way. You don't just buy stocks because someone on social media urged you to; you conduct your research.

Ask yourself: What does the company do? Is it growing? What is its track record? Successful investors do not risk; they strategize. Just like you develop your barbering skills, you must also refine your financial plan. The more knowledge you possess, the more confident and successful you will be.

Real wealth isn't created overnight, despite the fact that our world moves quickly. Building wealth through the stock market takes time, just as it did to become an expert barber. Avoid becoming sucked into the pursuit of easy money. Long-term growth is the focus of the stock market. You have a larger chance of seeing your investments increase the longer you play the game. Some of the wealthiest people become wealthy by staying in the market long enough to watch their money grow, not by timing the market precisely. It's similar to becoming known as a premier barber. It takes time and regular, high-quality labor to achieve; it doesn't happen after a single cut. Investing is no different. You must commit to the long term.

When it comes to investing, patience is essential. Although the stock market has a history of producing strong returns over time, it can be turbulent in the short term. The secret is to maintain your discipline, continue making contributions to your assets, and take advantage of compound interest. Your money will start to increase dramatically with time and consistency, albeit it might not happen right away.

The Cost of Inaction

The fact is that you are losing money if you are not investing. For a period. Although it may seem safe, keeping all of your money in a savings account is actually dangerous. Inflation is eroding your money while it is sitting there. Every year, your purchasing power decreases. Let's turn that now. Despite all of its volatility, the stock market has historically yielded returns of between 7–10% per year. That is the distinction between stagnating and progressing. Instead of letting your money sit around, you need to put it in a position to grow. Consider your finances as a team. You have two options: either put them in the game, where they have an opportunity to develop, score, and win, or let them sit on the bench and get weaker and weaker. By investing in the stock market, you may offer your money the chance to grow.

The consequences of not investing are real and get worse with time. You're losing out on possible growth and returns each year when you let your money sit inactively. As barbers, we understand the value of every dollar, so it's like leaving money on the table. Therefore, why not invest that money and allow it to begin working for you?

Building Wealth vs. Making Money

To be clear, this is about more than just increasing revenue. The goal is to accumulate riches. The two are very different from one another. Wealth is what you build for the future, not how much money you make today. Freedom, choice, and security are the hallmarks of wealth. It's about building a future in which you live the life you've always imagined rather than constantly working. When you make prudent investments, you're laying the groundwork for your family's future generations as well as for yourself. You are making something that will last beyond your lifetime. That's where investing truly shines.

It's what separates creating a legacy from merely having a job. Having money allows you to make decisions, take chances, and design the life you desire. The chances, experiences, and freedom that come with wealth are more important than the amount of money in your bank account.

Giving your loved ones that riches is more than just giving them cash; it means providing them the means to become financially independent on their own.

I understand what you're thinking, though: "But I have no idea what the stock market is all about. How should I make investments? I understand that, particularly for those who are unfamiliar with it, the stock market can appear daunting. Let me tell you, though, it's not as difficult as it looks. The secret is to be patient, conduct your homework, and start small. Using index funds is one of the simplest methods to get started. The performance of a broad market index, such as the S&P 500, is tracked by these funds. Without having to choose particular stocks, they're a fantastic method to gain exposure to the stock market. They also have a lengthy history of reliable returns and are usually inexpensive.

Using a robo-advisor is an additional choice. These are online investment systems that design and manage your portfolio according to your risk tolerance and goals using algorithms. You don't need to be an expert to get started because they take care of all the research and adjustments.

Simply taking the initial step is crucial. Even if you start off little, investing $50 a month, you're making an investment and developing the habit of generating wealth. Additionally, you can begin to increase the size of your portfolio and get more involved in your investment as you gain more knowledge and familiarity.

The Time to Act is Now

The truth is that waiting is the biggest mistake you can make. Yesterday was the finest time to begin investing but now is the second-best time. Being an expert is not necessary. Thousands of dollars are not necessary. All you need is the discipline to persevere, the patience to play the long game, and the willingness to learn. One of the best ways to increase your wealth is to invest in the stock market, but you must be prepared to make that commitment. Growth is never comfortable, but it won't always be at first. Therefore, consider this: will you continue to allow your money to sit and depreciate? Or will you take charge and use your finances to your advantage? Now is your time. It's time to enter the field, which is the stock market. You may create money that transforms not only your life but also the lives of your family members for many generations to come provided you have the correct attitude, plan, and commitment.

You're losing more time the longer you wait. You lose out on possible growth and rewards every day that your money is not invested. Therefore, stop putting things off, stop letting fear stop you, and start acting. With the correct strategy, the stock market may be your greatest partner in creating the life and legacy you deserve, despite its intimidating appearance. Although it may seem overwhelming, I can assure you that the benefits outweigh the risks. Imagine having a comfortable retirement, purchasing the home of your dreams, or preparing your children for success. That is the strength of stock market investing. Creating the life you desire on your own terms is more important than merely earning money.

What're you waiting for, then? It's time to start investing in your future and take the first step. Your 65-year-old self will appreciate it, I promise. One investment at a time, let's go to work and begin creating that riches.

John's Journey

Let us look at things from John's perspective, he was used to stash up his money but was able to get oriented about that mentality through a finance seminar that he attended. After attending that seminar, John had an epiphany, he had been playing small. He learned about investing in index funds, researched dividend stocks, and slowly built his portfolio. John implemented what he learned throughout the course of the seminar becoming a business owner with multiple income streams. His investments provided him with the financial cushion to expand his shop, offer new services, and even mentor younger barbers. His wealth wasn't just growing—it was multiplying.

Summary of Key Takeaways

- Making money while you sleep allows you to break free from trading time for cash.
- Inflation erodes your money's worth, making investing a necessity, not an option.
- You wouldn't cut a client's hair blindly, don't invest blindly either.
- John's success story proves that small steps lead to major results. Start investing today, and your wealth will multiply over time.
- The best time to start investing was yesterday. The second-best time is now. The longer you wait, the more you miss out on compounding returns.

The accumulation of wealth is a process that takes place day by day. With each investment, with each self-controlled spending, and with every new piece of information you acquire, you inch closer to financial independence. We barber put in a lot of time and effort for our clients' money; now it's time for that money to reward us.

Now is the moment to begin. If you put off taking advantage of compound interest, it will cost you more in the long run. Own your financial destiny, put your money where your mouth is, and see it grow exponentially. You should be able to decide for yourself whether or not you want to stand behind the chair, but it will always be there.

Revision Questions

1. You just finished a 12-hour shift at your barbershop, and you've made $1,000. How can you split this money between your needs, savings, and investments to maximize your long-term wealth?

    - What percentage should go into your investment portfolio?

    - How much should be saved for short-term goals?

- How can you reinvest in your business while still growing your personal wealth?

____
____
____
____
____
____
____
____
____
____
____
____
____
____

2. Imagine you had an opportunity to invest in stocks, real estate, or a high-interest savings account. Which would you choose and why?

- What are the risks and rewards of each option?
- How does your investment timeline impact your decision?
- What research steps would you take before investing?

____
____
____
____
____
____
____
____
____
____
____
____
____
____

3. Think about John's story. If you were in his shoes, what steps would you take today to ensure a better financial future five years from now?

    - How can you apply what John did to your own wealth-building strategy?
    - What habits would you need to change to reach financial independence?
    - What's stopping you from making your first investment today?

____

____

____

____

____

____

____

____

____

____

____

____

____

____

4. Many barbers believe in the "stack cash" mentality, avoiding investing out of fear. What are some common fears about investing, and how can you overcome them?

    - Have you ever been afraid to invest? Why?
    - What resources or knowledge could help you feel more confident?
    - What's one action step you can take today to start investing?

____

____

____

____

____

____

____

____

____

____

____

____

____

____

5. Picture yourself five years from now. What does financial success look like for you?

   - How much money do you want in your investment portfolio?
   - What kind of lifestyle do you want to build?
   - What steps can you take today to turn that vision into reality?

____

____

____

____

____

____

____

____

____

____

____

____

____

____

6. A client tells you he doesn't trust the stock market and prefers to keep his money in cash. How would you explain the impact of inflation to him in simple terms?

    - How would you compare inflation to something relatable (like hair clippers losing value)?

- What examples can you give him to show how investing beats inflation?

- What advice would you offer to help him start investing wisely?

CHAPTER 4

The Value Investing Barber

"The stock market is filled with individuals who know the price of everything but the value of nothing." – Philip Fisher

The Art of Value Investing

Barbers, my journey from a career in hairstyling to one of sustainable income creation began with a mentality shift, and I want to share that with you. Value investing is the craft I'm referring to. Now, before you lose interest because you believe this is irrelevant Wall Street jargon, allow me to explain it in a way that you can understand.

Just picture yourself able to channel your laser-like concentration into the stock market, just as you have done with your clippers. Improving your investment skills can lead to a more secure financial future, much like honing your cutting skills can lead to a perfectly styled client. Just like you've perfected your craft as a barber, value investing demands a dedication to understanding the fundamentals and a willingness to put in the hard work.

So, how does value investing work precisely? Consider this, it's easy to see if a customer has been maintaining a regular haircut routine or has been slacking off when they step foot in your salon. No doubt that some cuts call for greater effort than others. A client's lack of polish should in no way be taken as an indication of their lack of promise. A skilled barber may recognize the value under the surface and convert that client with a little effort. That's exactly what value investors do with equities.

Finding hidden gems, or stocks that are undervalued by the market but have the potential to increase in value over time, is the main goal of value investing. It's about looking past the obvious and figuring out when a business is worth much more than its current valuation. Consider Walmart (WMT) as an example. Although the stock's intrinsic value was predicted to be over $160 per share in 2020, it was trading at about $120 per share. When the market caught up to Walmart's actual value, value investors who understood its genuine worth were able to purchase the stock at a bargain and watch it increase over time.

And you don't rush value investing the way you don't rush a haircut. It all comes down to waiting patiently for the stock to realize its full potential. The best value investors are aware that long-term, steady, focused investing is the path to actual prosperity, rather than short-term speculation or get-rich-quick schemes.

Focusing on Intrinsic Value

Similar to how every client has a secret style that is just waiting to be unveiled and improved, every stock has a true value. This "intrinsic value," or a company's true value derived from its sound financial standing and core competencies, is what value investors concentrate on. To put it another way, what is the company's true value rather than what the market now claims it is worth?

To put it another way, picture yourself holding a high-end clipper that you know is $300. Now, you would be quick to take advantage of it if someone offered it to you for $50 since they are unsure of its actual worth. Why? since you are aware of its true value. Purchasing stocks that are trading below their true value is the essence of value investing. It all comes down to seeing a company's latent potential and having the patience to wait for the market to realize it.

The margin of safety is among the most crucial ideas in value investing. That built-in buffer shields you from risk when you purchase a stock at a bargain; it's similar to making sure you're wearing the appropriate protection before you start cutting. You're still receiving a terrific value while ensuring that there is some margin for mistake.

Suppose you purchase stock in a corporation that is valued at $100 per share, but the market price is $60. That difference of forty dollars? Your margin of safety is that.

You're allowing for contingencies in case the market changes or something goes wrong. You know that you're still in the game even if you need to make some modifications, so it's like giving yourself more time to polish that fade. One important risk-management strategy used by investors to safeguard their capital is this margin of safety.

The Long-Term Perspective

Value investment is similar to barbering in this regard; it's all about the long term. It takes more than two minutes to give a customer a flawless haircut. It requires patience, accuracy, and a steady hand. Value investing is no exception. You want to steadily increase your wealth over time, not make rapid flips or fall for get-rich-quick schemes.

After investing in a business at a bargain, you must wait for it to reach its full potential. The beauty of this procedure is that it takes time to mature. You're not attempting to forecast the next big thing or follow trends. While you continue honing your skills behind the chair, you're investing in reliable businesses and letting them handle the work for you. Your patience and discipline in allowing your investments to compound over time will yield the real benefits of value investing.

Basic Analysis

You wouldn't enter the financial market without doing your research, just as you wouldn't enter a barbershop without understanding how to cut. The secret to value investing is fundamental examination. It's similar to examining a client's head shape before beginning a scalp examination or cutting. You must be aware of what you are dealing with.

Fundamental analysis involves examining a company's financials, including cash flow, earnings, leadership caliber, and how the business compares to its competitors. It's similar to inspecting the tools you use on a daily basis; you're not only looking at the outside; you're also evaluating the durability and performance to make sure it's a reliable tool.

Just because everyone is talking about a stock doesn't mean you should buy it. Investigate. Does the business make money? Are they becoming bigger? Are they ahead of the competition? Consider it like choosing the appropriate trimmer or clipper for the task. The outcomes will speak for themselves if you make the correct decision and use the appropriate method. What distinguishes effective value investors from others who only follow the newest trends is this depth of knowledge.

One characteristic that sets value investors apart from the rest is their willingness to defy expectations. The greatest possibilities occasionally present themselves when everyone else is sleeping on them. Similar to when a client arrives with a vintage look that everyone else may consider out of style, but you see the opportunity to bring it back to its former glory.

Value investors frequently make investments in underperforming businesses or industries. Value investors wait patiently for the market to recognize the worth of an undervalued stock while everyone else chases the latest, trendy fad. Just because a style isn't popular right now doesn't imply it won't be in the future. It's similar to cutting your hair. When the chance arises, you must be willing to defy expectations and have faith in your research and gut feelings.

Maintaining Self-Control

Let's be honest: just like in the store, there is always noise in the market. However, if you're a good barber, you don't allow distractions ruin your work. Investing is no different. There will be fluctuations, but if you have done your homework and made a wise investment, you must maintain your composure and resist the urge to be swayed by transient market fluctuations. Discipline and patience are key components of value investing. Like a complex mind full of swirls and curls, the market will challenge you, but you must have faith in your method and allow time and ability to work in your advantage. Keep in mind that your goal is not to make rapid money. You're a barber who builds riches, so you're creating something more than that.

It's time to start considering how we can make those dollars work for us, even if barbers are aware of the hardship of working hard for every dollar. Value investing allows you to start accumulating wealth for the future rather than merely making money now. It's about building a future in which your income increases even when you don't make any cuts.

Consider the conglomerate Berkshire Hathaway (BRK.A), which is run by renowned value investor Warren Buffett. A $1,000 investment has grown to over $27 million thanks to Berkshire's shares, which has increased by over 2,700,000% over the last 50 years. Finding undervalued businesses with solid fundamentals and allowing them to grow your wealth over time is the magic of value investing done correctly. Value investment allows you to lead the path rather than just follow the pack. Where others see no opportunities, you see them. Just as you take charge of the clippers in your hand, you are also taking charge of your financial destiny.

This goes beyond simple investing. It's about developing your wealth-building skills with the same level of accuracy, focus, and perseverance that you apply to your daily work. Now is the moment, barbers. Let's begin investing and paving the way for financial independence.

John's Growth Through Value Investing

Let me tell you about John, the barber whose story you've been following. After learning stock investing, John recognized he needed a smarter technique to pick his investments. He started studying value investing, looking for stocks that were inexpensive but had excellent financial fundamentals.

He spotted a company that reminded him of an old, devoted client who had stopped coming in for regular cuts. The business had good operations but was briefly disregarded. Instead of ignoring it, John saw an opportunity. He invested, waited patiently, and watched as the stock progressively soared. Within a few years, John's portfolio had risen significantly—not because he followed the trends, but because he invested properly.

Summary of Key Takeaways

- Value investing is like barbering—patience and skill lead to the best results.
- Intrinsic value is key—look beyond market price to find hidden gems.
- The best investments take time to mature—rushed moves rarely lead to lasting wealth.
- John's success proves that focusing on long-term, high-quality investments leads to major gains.
- Stay disciplined—don't let short-term market noise distract you from building wealth.

Now is the time to sharpen not only your clippers but your financial mindset. Start identifying undervalued opportunities in both your career and investments. Wealth is built by those who see value where others don't.

Revision Questions

1. Imagine you're evaluating stocks as if you were evaluating clients. What key qualities would you look for before making a decision?

    - How do you identify a strong company beyond just its stock price?
    - What financial indicators are similar to how you assess the quality of a client's hair before a cut?

____

____

____

____

____

____

____

____

____

____

____

____

____

____

2. You have $5,000 to invest and must choose between a high-growth tech stock and an undervalued blue-chip company. How do you decide?

    - What are the risks and rewards of each?

    - How does value investing help lower risk?

____

____

____

____

____

____

____

____

____

____

____

____

____

____

3. Think about John's journey. How would his story have changed if he had ignored value investing and chased trends instead?

    - How do trends mislead investors?
    - Why do patient investors often succeed more than impulsive ones?

____

____

____

____

____

____

____

____

____

____

____

____

____

____

4. Picture your future financial freedom. How does value investing fit into your long-term wealth-building plan?

    - What percentage of your portfolio would you dedicate to value stocks?

    - How would you reinvest dividends and gains?

____

____

____

____

____

____

____

____

____

____

____

____

____

____

5. Explain to a friend why understanding intrinsic value is crucial when investing.

    - How would you use the example of undervalued clippers or tools to explain the concept?

    - What happens when people buy stocks based on hype rather than actual value?

____

____

____

____

____

____

____

____

____

____

____

____

____

____

6. If you had to apply the principles of value investing to your own barbershop business, how would you do it?

   - How can you spot undervalued opportunities in your own industry?

   - What business strategies align with the patient, long-term mindset of value investing?

____

____

CHAPTER 5

The Wealth-Building Barber's Key to Success: Building and Retaining a Clientele

"People will forget what you said, they will forget what you did, but they will never forget how you made them feel." - Maya Angelou

Developing wealth as a barber involves more than simply your bank account and stock market investments. Your clientele is your first and most important investment, and it's far more basic. You'll be working day in and day out, fighting for every dollar that comes in the door, if you don't have a solid, devoted clientele. However, you will be able to access steady cash flow that may be carefully directed toward wealth-building opportunities if you become an expert at drawing in, fostering, and keeping a loyal customer.

Building a customer involves more than just cutting hair; it also entails developing trust, establishing relationships, and providing exceptional value outside of the chair. Your customers are the cornerstone of your financial success; they are more than just appointments. You have greater control over your income, your schedule, and ultimately your future if your customer is larger and more devoted. Let's dissect the effective tactics that will enable you to establish and maintain this crucial base.

Hand-to-Hand Combat: The Influence of Human Relationships

Success in barbershops has always been closely tied to interpersonal connections. Barbers were establishing their clientele through what I like to refer to as "hand-to-hand combat"—meeting people in person, establishing a personal connection, and fostering trust—long before social media and advanced marketing. This approach is still one of the best methods to expand your company and is just as applicable now as it was decades ago.

You have to work hard when you're first starting out. This include exchanging cards (digital or real), shaking hands, and introducing yourself. However, distributing business cards alone is insufficient; the true magic occurs during follow-up. Too many barbers have stopped distributing cards and are now relying on customers to find them. Instead, contact information can be instantly gathered using contemporary methods like SlickText or comparable services. For instance, offer prospective customers a 50% discount on their first haircut if they text "CUT" to a designated number, which will allow them to access your photo gallery. In addition to encouraging people to stop by your store, this also records their name, phone number, and email address so you can keep up the conversation even beyond the initial meet-and-greet.

There's always a chance to strike up a discussion with a possible customer, whether you're in the grocery store, the gym, or a social gathering. The secret, though, is to build rapport before pitching your services. Until others realize how much you care, they won't care how much you know.

Individuals do business with people they trust, like, and know. Saying something like, "Hey, come to my shop so I can give you a great cut," while holding out a card, puts your needs before of theirs. Instead, focus on them, discuss their grooming practices, and show interest in their sense of style. "To sell to Mr. Jones what Mr. Jones buys, you must first see things through Mr. Jones' eyes," I frequently say to my students and barbers.

Recognize that customers are purchasing answers to their problems rather than goods or services. When someone purchases a T-shirt, they are purchasing a message or a sense of comfort rather than fabric. When someone purchases eyeglasses, they are purchasing improved vision rather than plastic and metal. What are your customers actually purchasing, then? A hairstyle? No. They are purchasing self-assurance, self-worth, and a dependable service they can rely on. Convenience, professionalism, and trust are what they are buying.

Every encounter is a chance to acquire a customer and make extra money. Never ignore a possible customer without establishing a rapport. Tell them you're there to make them feel and look their best, introduce yourself, and lead with value. Every person in your chair represents a possible source of income. The money will come if you concentrate on meeting their requirements and going above and beyond for them.

The John Story

John, the barber we've been following up, also had the issue of irregular customer. He relied primarily on walk-ins and never formed significant ties with his clientele. As a result, his income varied, and he had little control over his financial future.

After learning about personal branding and value-based service, John revolutionized his firm. He didn't simply cut hair, he knew his clients' names, asked about their families, and made them feel important. He devised a referral scheme, rewarding people to bring in their friends. In just two years,

John moved from barely making ends meet to having a completely packed calendar with dedicated customers who wouldn't let anybody else touch their hair.

What changed? John stopped thinking like merely a barber and started thinking like a businessman. He understood that the most successful barbers don't just cut hair, they establish relationships that lead into generational wealth.

The Revolution of Word-of-Mouth

The barber profession relies heavily on word-of-mouth referrals. Although social media is fantastic, it will never be able to match the effectiveness of real recommendations. A customer becomes an advocate for your brand as they leave your chair. Their remarks are your most effective marketing weapon, and their new cut is your walking billboard.

The fact is that people have faith in one another. You have a terrific opportunity when a client receives a great cut and their friends or complete strangers ask, "Who did that for you?" It is your responsibility to ensure that each and every client you work with feels as though they have had the most fulfilling experience of their lives. It's all about consistency, word-of-mouth must be earned; it cannot be coerced. It is the result of your abilities, expertise, and experience. Whether it's your meticulous attention to detail, your spotless surroundings, or your regard for their time, people will talk when you give them something to talk about.

Do you want to increase word-of-mouth marketing? Provide rewards. Give your customers an incentive to recommend you to others. Offer discounts for recommendations, for instance, or give your most devoted customers VIP treatment. They will eagerly refer new customers to your chair if you can make it valuable for them.

Social Media as The New Digital Barbershop

Social media sites like Facebook, Instagram, and TikTok are the new storefronts in the modern world. You're losing money if you're not making use of these resources. But keep in mind that social media is a platform for developing your brand and drawing in upscale customers, not just a place to flaunt your cuts. Your digital portfolio is your Instagram page. In addition to showcasing your work, each piece should explain why prospective clients should pick you above the competition. The experience, atmosphere, and way of life that come with sitting on your chair are more important than the cut alone.

On social media, consistency is essential. Invite others into your environment, share your greatest work, and post frequently. Display your shop's enthusiasm, your client interactions, and your barbering adventure. Allowing others in fosters relationships that go well beyond the screen. Interact with your followers by DMing possible customers, leaving comments, and striking up discussions. You will become more visible the more active you are. Social media is only the hook, though. When your followers turn into devoted customers, the true magic occurs. It's your responsibility to provide an experience that will entice them to return once they're in your chair.

The Barbershop Experience Beyond the Cut

A fantastic haircut is only the first step. When was the last time you visited a business and had a memorable experience? The emotion you had when you left was more important than the actual product. Your clients are no different.

Are you offering an experience, or are you just giving them a haircut? Each and every detail counts, from the time they enter until they depart. Keep in mind their names, their backstories, and their inclinations. While customers wait, provide a drink, maintain a clean store, and make sure the music and ambiance are appropriate. Clients will return for more than just the cut when you make the effort to create a memorable experience.

The True Secret Behind Wealth Retention

While bringing in new customers is important, building wealth comes from keeping existing ones. While one-time customers are fantastic, what about recurring ones? The real money can be found there. Recurring customers translate into steady paychecks. They give you the ability to forecast your earnings, establish financial security, and lay a solid basis for accumulating wealth.

Consistency is the first step toward retention. Regardless of whether it's their first or hundredth visit, make sure each customer feels like they're receiving the greatest care possible. Always go above and beyond what they anticipate Maintain communication with your customers. During the holidays, check in, send reminder SMS, and provide loyalty programs or exclusive offers. People will continue to return when they feel valued.

In the end, your clientele serves as the cornerstone of all your barbering endeavors. A devoted customer base generates steady revenue flow, which enables you to make investments in your future. You will become more financially independent the more you put into acquiring and keeping customers. And that independence gives you access to chances to build money you never would have thought possible.

Keep in mind that every customer you draw in, every experience you produce, and every connection you make is a step toward financial success rather than merely a service. You're creating a legacy rather than just cutting hair when you concentrate on developing and keeping a loyal customer. And that's the real indicator of a barber who builds riches.

Let me conclude by saying that your clients are your partners in creating wealth, not just your clients. They will reward you with their loyalty, recommendations, and ongoing business if you treat them as such. They will invest in you if you invest in them. That's the key to realizing your barbershop's full potential and achieving the financial independence you are due.

Summary of Key Takeaways

- Your clientele is your most valuable asset.
- Word-of-mouth marketing is more powerful than any ad campaign.
- Social media is your digital storefront—use it wisely.
- Loyal clients generate stable, long-term wealth.
- Create an experience, not just a haircut.
- John's transformation proves that personal branding and relationship-building are crucial.

Your barbershop is more than a business; it's a legacy in the making. Develop relationships, master retention, and watch your wealth develop beyond the chair.

Revision Questions

1. Think about your top five clients. What keeps them coming back? How can you replicate that experience for all clients?

    - What specific service or interaction makes your barbershop stand out?

    - How can you enhance client loyalty?

____

____

____

____

____

____

____

____

____

____

____

____

____

____

2. Imagine you just moved to a new city with zero clients. How would you build your clientele from scratch?

    - What marketing strategies would you use?

    - How would you establish trust with first-time clients?

____

____

____

____

____

____

____

____

____

____

____

____

____

____

3. You have two choices: spend $1,000 on social media ads or invest it in a referral program. Which is the better investment and why?

    - What are the pros and cons of each?

    - How can word-of-mouth be amplified through digital marketing?

____

____

____

____

____

____

____

____

____

____

____

____

____

____

4. John doubled his clientele in two years by focusing on relationships. If you had to adopt one of his strategies, which would it be? Why?

    - What changes can you make today to improve client retention?

____

____

____

____

____

____

____

____

____

____

5. How can you leverage your personal brand to attract premium clients willing to pay higher prices?

    - What elements of your branding stand out?
    - How can you position yourself as the go-to barber in your community?

____

____

____

____

____

6. What's stopping you from implementing loyalty programs, VIP services, or additional income streams today?

    - What small step can you take right now?
    - How can you ensure steady income outside of just cutting hair?

____

____

____

____

____

____

____

____

____

____

____

____

____

____

CHAPTER 6

Building Your Financial Portfolio

"Money is a great servant but a terrible master. If you don't put it to work, it will work against you." – Unknown

Barbers do more than just cut hair; they also mold people's confidence, style, and identity. Beyond the chair, every barber must learn how to make riches. You must sharpen your financial game just as you sharpen your tools on a daily basis. Every investment you make is a tool that, when utilized effectively, will shape your financial future in the same way that you influence your customers' appearance. This chapter isn't just about investing; it's about putting your money to work for you long after you've put away the clippers.

Just for a second, picture a barbershop as your portfolio. Any time you put money into your business, it's like adding a new service or employee to your roster. You shouldn't expect your investments to behave in the same manner as each individual barber on your staff, just as you wouldn't want your employees to all wear matching haircuts. To achieve both stability and growth, you need a strategic blend, or a team whose members complement one another.

Here we'll discuss the basics of starting a "wealth-building shop" in the stock market, the importance of age in determining financial success, and why now could be a good time to start, particularly for young barbers just starting out.

Why Does Age Matter?

Time is your best friend when it comes to investing. When you're young, you have one of the most powerful tools in finance on your side: compound growth. In plain terms, that means the money you invest today has time to grow, and then that growth can grow, and so on. Think of it like this: the younger you are, the more time you have for your money to build upon itself - just like mastering the perfect drop fade takes practice and consistency, so does building wealth.

If you've ever instructed a new barber, you know that it takes time for them to learn even the most basic methods. They struggle at first, but with enough repetition, their skills build up, and they're cutting with confidence. Your investments operate in the same way. When you start early, your money grows organically, helping you to achieve financial security with less worry and work. But if you wait, you'll be playing catch-up, much like a barber who realizes too late that speed and quality must go hand in hand.

Here's the rule: the more time your money spends in the market, the greater your potential returns. When you're in the 18-35 age range, you don't need every dollar to work for you immediately, which gives you the flexibility to weather market ups and downs. Just as you might tell a client they need to be patient to grow out that perfect style, time is essential for growing wealth. As you age, your approach needs to adjust since your financial needs become more immediate, and stability becomes a greater concern.

The Ideal Age to Start Investing

When you're between 18 and 35, you have the perfect blend of time, flexibility, and potential. Here's why: at this age, your financial commitments might be lower. Maybe you're not yet responsible for family expenses, mortgage payments, or the bulk of retirement planning. This is your chance to let your money grow in the background.

In your twenties or early thirties, you also have time on your side to bounce back if (or rather when) the market dips. Because the market will crash, it's part of the game. But those who understand the rules of the game know that downturns are temporary and that staying consistent brings the reward. For barbers in this age range, the key is to start and stay invested, even if you can only put aside a small amount at first. Just as you might gradually add new services or products to your shop, every little bit you add to your investments will eventually multiply.

The Power of Starting Early: A Real-Life Comparison

To paint a clearer picture, let's break it down:

- Example 1: Let's say you choose to invest $200 a month until you are 65 years old. You will have about $535,000 when you retire, assuming an annual return of 7%. Just by making little, regular investments over time, that's half a million dollars.

- Example 2: Now, suppose you started that same $200 monthly investment with the same 7% return at age 35. By the time you reach 65, you will have roughly $244,000. Although it's still good, it's less than half of what you would have if you had begun ten years earlier.

For this reason, the best wealth-building tip is to start today, while you're still young. Young investments position you for future success, not only for yourself but also for future generations. It's similar to honing a skill early in your profession.

John's Portfolio Shift

John, who had previously struggled to see beyond the daily grind of cutting hair, began paying attention to the wealthiest clients who sat in his chair." He saw that they all shared one thing in common: investments. They weren't simply working for money; their money was working for them. Inspired, John established a goal: to build an investing portfolio that would one day eliminate his need to sit behind a desk entirely. He started modestly, investing $100 each month in an index fund. He then put his excess income in rental houses. John gradually leveraged his haircut earnings into a financial safety net, allowing him to retire comfortably. His barbershop was no longer just a source of income; it was an asset that he might sell or pass down in the future.

Building Your Portfolio: A Barber's Guide

You are aware of the need of a well-balanced blend while cutting hair. It requires a combination of expertise, accuracy, and tools; you can't just leave one portion of the head unblended and hope it works itself out. This is also true while building a stock portfolio. You want a mix of investments that strike a balance between security and development.

Here are some things to think about:

- Growth Stocks: Growth stocks are great potential but occasionally dangerous, much like the ambitious young barbers in your shop. They stand for businesses that are rapidly growing and have the potential to yield large profits, but they also carry a higher degree of volatility.

- Dividend Stocks: Dividend stocks are like the dependable barbers that consistently attract the same clientele. Even while they might not grow as quickly, they nevertheless give you a stable income, much like dividends do, which helps you gradually accumulate money over time.

- I ndex funds and ETFs: they make up a strong, dependable team. They provide equilibrium and cover a large portion of the market. Because index funds and exchange-traded funds (ETFs) track whole segments of the market, your money is dispersed over several businesses, lowering the chance that you will lose it all at once.

- Bonds: Consider bonds to be the sturdy, long-lasting chairs in your shop that hold everything else up. They offer security rather than rapid returns, particularly when you approach the time when you will need that money for retirement.

You don't get results right away when you plant seeds. It requires patience, nurture, and attention. It's the same with becoming a barber who builds wealth. Although a well-designed portfolio takes time to grow, you may position yourself for financial success by continuously "watering" it with modest, consistent investments.

Developing into a wealth-building barber requires putting the long term ahead of daily profits. It's about leaving a financial legacy for future generations as well as for your family, community, and yourself. Start now, even if it's only a little, and see how you develop not only as a barber but also as a leader, investor, and money creator.

You may be unfamiliar with this path, but it's only another ability to learn. And keep in mind that consistency, patience, and an eye for growth are the true keys, just as when cutting hair.

Summary of Key Takeaways

- Start investing early, time is your greatest advantage.
- Diversify your portfolio like a well-run barbershop.
- Let your money work for you instead of sitting idle in a savings account.
- Real estate and stock investments create passive income, reducing dependence on cutting hair alone.
- John's journey shows that investing transforms financial security and creates generational wealth.

Building a financial portfolio isn't about getting rich quick—it's about getting rich for sure. A barber with a strong portfolio isn't just working for today, he's securing tomorrow. Start today, invest wisely, and watch your wealth compound like a well-crafted barbering career. Your future self will thank you!

Revision Questions

1. You just earned an extra $10,000 from increased clientele. What's your plan for that money?

    - How much will you invest vs. reinvest into your shop?
    - What investment options make the most sense for your goals?

____

____

____

____

____

____

____

____

____

____

____

____

____

____

2. Your client tells you they don't trust investing and prefer to keep cash. How do you explain why investing is smarter?

    - What analogies could help them understand?
    - How does inflation impact cash over time?

____

____

____

____

____

____

____

____

____

____

____

____

____

____

3. John used small investments to build wealth. What's one step you can take today to start doing the same?

   - Could you automate monthly investments?
   - What asset class interests you most?

____

____

____

____

____

____

____

____

____

____

____

____

____

____

4. Imagine your portfolio five years from now. What does success look like?

    - How diversified will your investments be?
    - What actions will you take today to ensure you're on track?

____

____

____

____

____

____

____

____

____

____

____

____

____

____

5. If you had to choose between investing in real estate, stocks, or expanding your barbershop, which would you choose and why?

    - How does each option align with your financial goals?
    - What risks and rewards come with each choice?

____

____

____

____

____

____

____

____

____

____

____

____

____

____

6. How can you transition from thinking about money as income to thinking about it as a tool for wealth-building?

    - What mindset shifts are necessary to start seeing money differently?

    - How can you start making money work for you instead of working for money?

____

____

____

____

____

____

____

____

____

____

____

____

____

____

CHAPTER 7

The Wealth-Building Barber's Guide to Achieving Financial Freedom

"Don't wait to buy real estate. Buy real estate and wait." – Will Rogers

The sound of clippers and talk fills your barbershop every day. Clients bring stories, connections, issues, and goals of their own when they sit in your chair; they are not only there for a new haircut. The problem is that practically all of your clients share the urge for a place to call home. Everyone needs a place to live, whether it's a house they may own or rent. You have a huge potential because of this need. Imagine using the folks you already assist as the cornerstone for your wealth-building initiative. This chapter discusses how you, as a proficient barber with a clientele, might use real estate to further your barbering business's prosperity.

Buy and Hold: Turning Clients into Renters (and Passive Cash Flow)

Imagine a client who visits for a cut every two weeks. They spend between $40 and $100 per visit, and if handled well, that sum of money builds up over time. Imagine if in addition to paying for your haircuts, they are also covering your rent. That is the strength of purchasing and owning real estate.

Imagine after you've built trust with your clients over time. They come to you for more than just haircuts; they also seek guidance and chat. Consider this: one of those clients is looking for a place to rent. Rather than simply trimming their hair, you become their landlord. They trust you, and you offer them with an excellent living environment while earning a consistent passive income. Your shop still generates revenue, but you now have a second stream of income operating in the background, paying your mortgage and increasing your wealth. The idea is to think about tomorrow's ownership rather than today's transaction.

Buying and holding is the process of buying a property, renting it out, and allowing it to bring in money each month. People from various walks of life, including many in need of rental accommodation, frequent your barbershop. Many of the prospective tenants in your network already have faith in you. In addition to creating financial security, you're also fostering a sense of community within your real estate endeavors by renting to people you know and who appreciate your services.

Think about these advantages:

- Familiar Tenants: You have strong ties to your community because you work as a barber. You probably know reliable people in need of a decent place to reside. Renting from customers or through recommendations from customers lowers your risk because you are already familiar with their reputation and character.

- Consistent Cash Flow: Renters give your barbershop a continuous flow of cash, much like a steady stream of customers brings in money. Your rental income builds equity for you while paying off the mortgage each month. This implies that you can accumulate wealth without getting your hair cut.

Imagine each property being a chair in your store that brings in money, but one that doesn't require breaks, has no sick days, and doesn't depend on your time. By buying and holding, you can develop money over time, create automatic cash flow, and feel more at ease.

Wholesaling Real Estate - Making Deals Like You're Connecting Clients

Wholesale real estate has the advantage of not requiring you to have a license, good credit, or a lot of money. Literally, you could begin right now. We barbers are familiar with the hustle of making things happen with what we have, and wholesaling real estate is no different. You do not have to be the property's owner in order to engage in wholesale. You are merely the go-between, bringing together investors who wish to purchase real estate and sellers. You're generating a lucrative opportunity through your networking, much like when you introduce two clients who could profit from one other's enterprises.

For instance:

- You uncover a $80,000 property and sign a $50,000 contract for it. You approach an investor who is involved in real estate investing or flipping, and offer them the contract for $60,000. You take home a $10,000 profit, and the investor benefits greatly. Now, depending on how you arranged the transaction, your profit might be considerably greater. Wholesale real estate was the first step taken by the majority of significant real estate tycoons to reach their current positions. After making a lot of money from their wholesale transactions, they began investing in fix-and-flip properties.

The benefit of wholesaling is that it is a tactic that naturally complements a barber's skill set. The key to wholesaling is timing, establishing connections, and knowing people, all of which you already excel at in the barbershop. Every discussion with a client has the potential to generate a lead. They may want to make their own investment or know someone who is selling real estate. Your chair turns into a center of opportunity, not only for haircuts but also for real estate transactions that have the power to change your financial situation.

John's Story

John had mastered the knack of keeping his barbershop busy. But as he got older, he realized something: he was still trading time for money. He needed a technique to earn money while sleeping. So he turned to real estate. His initial transaction was a small two-bedroom rental house. He didn't have all of the cash, but he used a bank loan to find a tenant, one of his long-term clients. That single home began paying for itself, covering its mortgage and gradually increasing in value. Encouraged by his achievement, John continued to invest. Over the next decade, he accumulated a portfolio of rental residences, all of which were occupied by referrals from his barbershop. What began with clippers and chats grew into an empire of passive income, allowing John to retire early and mentor the next generation of barbers.

Buying Tax Lien Properties

Properties with delinquent taxes are known as tax lien properties. Local governments are prepared to sell the property for pennies on the dollar in order to recoup those taxes. Imagine it as an undiscovered gem, a diamond in the rough, waiting for the proper person (you!) to recognize its potential.

This is yet another fantastic chance for a barber. You can obtain leads on houses with tax liens by reaching out to your current clientele. The benefits of this approach are enormous, but it does take some research and a thorough understanding of the market. This is the reason:

- Instant Value: Since you purchase these homes at a discount, you get equity right now. The property is typically worth more than you purchased, even if you don't make any modifications.

- Impact on the Community: Purchasing tax lien properties can contribute to neighborhood revitalization, enhancing not only your personal wealth but also the living and working conditions of you, your business, and your clients. Before others do it, you'll be able to gentrify your own neighborhood by buying by the block.

Suppose you pay $20,000 for a property that is worth $50,000 through a tax lien. You have $30,000 in equity right away, protecting your investment. You will have even more monthly cash flow if you choose to rent it out. When I first started investing in real estate, I ran into a problem where I was on the other side of this kind of scenario. Unbeknownst to me, I owed $2000 in property taxes on a $70,000 property that I owned outright. I could have lost a lot of money because of that one error or ignorance. In order to save my property, I had to pay an extra $4,800 in addition to the

$2000 in property taxes. That was a really important lesson. On the other hand, the investor on the other end of the spectrum was going to make a huge appearance ($68,000 in equity). You can print this kind of money in another game, please.

Understanding ARV: Never Overpay and Always Get the Best Deal

The After Repair Value (ARV) is a key idea in real estate that guarantees you're investing wisely. The worth of the property after upgrades is known as the ARV. You can determine just how much you should spend for a property by knowing this value up front, preventing you from taking on too much debt or losing money on a transaction.

The following guideline will help you stay profitable and simple:

- **Maximum Purchase Price = ARV x 70%**

For example, if the ARV of a property is $250,000, multiply that by 70% to get $175,000. This indicates that $175,000 is the most you should spend on both purchasing and renovating this home. By following this approach, you may be sure that your investment is secure and won't cause you to lose sleep about debt. Additionally, banks usually refinance at 70% of the ARV, allowing you to withdraw your original investment if necessary.

Think of this formula as your safety net; it's there to keep you safe and ensure that every home you purchase is a step up the financial ladder.

Using Real Estate to Build Wealth

Here is a detailed example of how you could use real estate to transform the earnings from your barbershop into long-term wealth:

1. You discover a rental home while you're conserving money and chopping hair.

2. Applying the 70% rule, you buy the property for less than its true value and lease it to a client in need of housing.

3. The rental income comes in each month, which helps build equity and pay down the mortgage.

4. You take money out of the refinance and put it into another property.

This approach of rinsing and repeating works well. Each step builds on the one before it, producing a snowball effect where the money from each property fuels the subsequent transaction. You'll soon be establishing an empire in addition to cutting hair.

As a barber, the true advantage of real estate investing is that you never have to start from nothing. Any customer who enters your business could be a potential tenant, a real estate lead, or even another investor. Every haircut you get at the barbershop feeds into your next move, creating a network of opportunities.

Consider the independence that comes from knowing that you are not dependent on a single source of money. A power that continues to work for you long after you've shut down your business for the day, real estate is a wealth multiplier. You can provide financial independence, security for your family, and an asset that can be passed down to future generations by accumulating a portfolio of real estate. As you proceed, keep in mind that your chair is a seat for many chances rather than just a spot to make cuts. You possess the customers, the contacts, and the motivation. It's now time to enter the real estate market, one house at a time.

Summary of Key Takeaways

- Your barbershop is your network. Leverage client relationships to find tenants, investment opportunities, and real estate deals.

- Real estate creates passive income. Unlike working behind the chair, rental income works for you 24/7.

- Wholesaling and tax liens are entry points. You don't need massive capital to start investing.

- ARV protects your investments. Follow the 70% rule to ensure long-term profitability.

- John's journey proves it's possible. Even with no prior experience, he turned a barbering career into a real estate empire.

Financial freedom starts when your money works harder than you do. Real estate is the vehicle and your shop is the engine. It's time to make your next move.

Revision Questions

1. You've saved $10,000 and want to invest in real estate. What's your first move?

    - Would you buy a rental property, wholesale a deal, or invest in tax liens?

    - What factors would influence your decision?

____

____

____

____

____

____

____

____

____

____

____

____

____

____

2. How can you use the relationships in your barbershop to find real estate deals?

    - What questions could you ask clients to uncover investment opportunities?

    - How can you network without being too aggressive?

____

____

____

____

____

____

____

____

____

____

____

---

3. John transitioned from barbering to real estate investing. How can you follow a similar path?

   - What's the first real estate move you could make?
   - What obstacles might you face, and how could you overcome them?

____

____

____

____

4. Imagine you own three rental properties generating $5,000 per month. How does that change your life?

- What freedoms does this income give you?
- How would you reinvest your profits to expand further?

____

____

____

____

____

____

____

____

____

____

____

____

____

____

5. What's your long-term financial vision?

- Where do you see yourself in 10 years?
- How does real estate fit into your wealth-building strategy?

____

____

____

____

____

____

____

____

____

____

____

____

____

____

6. What mindset shifts do you need to make to start investing?

    - Are there fears or doubts holding you back?
    - How can you overcome them to take action today?

____

____

____

____

____

____

____

____

____

CHAPTER 8

Mastering Client Retention for Long-Term Wealth

"A great haircut fades, but great service builds a lifetime of loyalty. Your clients are not just transactions, they're the foundation of your financial empire." - Unknown

The Barber's Guide to Building Lasting Client Relationships

Investing in your clientele is more valuable than buying a fancy chair, a new pair of clippers, or even a barbershop. To succeed in the long run, you need a steady stream of loyal clients. You will have to fight for every dollar every day without retention, and you won't have much of a safety net either.

But what draws in clients and keeps them coming back?

Customers spend more than just on a haircut. What they end up spending money on is:

- An amazing experience, one that boosts their self-esteem and makes them feel like they matter.

- Whether it's finding a superior fade, getting guidance from grooming experts, or simply finding an escape from daily stress, there's a solution for them.

- An attachment to a group - Barbershops are communities in and of themselves, not just businesses.

Without mastering client retention, even the best haircut abilities won't guarantee long-term success. If you want to convert from just making money to building wealth, you need to establish an environment where clients feel compelled to return—not just for your cuts, but for the experience and service you deliver.

The Barber's Competitive Advantage

If you can answer this one question, you'll never worry about client retention again:

"Why should a client choose me over any other barber?"

You must sell yourself before you offer your services. Clients aren't just purchasing a haircut, they're buying YOU.

This means you need to focus on your overall presence and service excellence. First and foremost, your character plays a key influence in retaining clients. Are you reliable, professional, and approachable? A client wants to feel comfortable in your chair, knowing that you are not only skilled but also someone they can trust with their look. Your skill level is another crucial component, consistency in producing high-quality outcomes is what turns first-time visitors into lifelong clients. Clients must trust that every time they arrange an appointment, they will receive a faultless cut that increases their confidence.

Beyond these, trustworthiness cannot be neglected. Clients respect a barber who listens to their demands, understands their style preferences, and makes competent ideas. They may not always articulate their concerns, but they will always notice the tiny things. Is your shop clean and well-maintained? Does the tone of your talk make them feel welcome and respected? Are you attentive to their specific haircut preferences? Most importantly, do you actively listen to their requirements and give unique solutions?

These simple yet important elements build a sense of trust and professionalism, reaffirming why clients should return to you rather than go elsewhere. Noticing the slightest things like recommending a scalp treatment when you sense dryness, shows that you care beyond simply the cut. This is how you transform one-time clients into lifetime clients.

Clients may not always express their worries overtly, but their loyalty is influenced by the little things they witness every time they enter your shop. The first thing they take in is the cleanliness of your desk. A pristine business shows professionalism, hygiene, and concern for both your trade and your clients. A well-maintained workplace reassures them that they are in excellent care, while a chaotic or unclean setting could make them think twice about returning.

Beyond the physical space, the tone of your interactions plays a key impact on their overall experience. Clients don't just come for a haircut, they also come for engagement. Whether it's a pleasant discussion, a professional counsel, or simply a serene, relaxing moment, your ability to read the room and alter your approach makes a lasting impact. Engaging in meaningful communication without overstepping personal boundaries lets clients feel heard and respected.

Additionally, your devotion to their tastes says volumes. Do you remember how they like their fade? Did you take note of a specific request from their last visit? These simple yet important details convey that you cherish their business beyond just a transaction. When clients feel like more than just another appointment in your book, they become devoted customers who trust you with their image and confidence.

Lastly, your ability to actually listen and offer solutions is what sets you apart from the regular barber. If a client expresses scalp irritation, do you recommend the proper items or services? If they express discontent with a previous cut, do you tweak and reassure them? Clients want to know they are in the hands of someone who not only listens to them but actually takes action to address their requirements. This level of attentiveness promotes trust and builds long-term connections that convert into financial success.

Overcoming Client Objections Like the wealth building barber

One of the greatest reasons barbers struggle to expand and retain their clients isn't a lack of skill, it's their inability to manage complaints correctly. When a client expresses worry about price, wait times, or even contemplates trying a different barber, they're not necessarily rejecting you. Instead, they're looking for reassurance that your service is worth their investment. A master barber doesn't run away from these objections; he transforms them into opportunities to establish deeper connections with clients.

Take pricing, for example. If a client says, "Your prices are too high," don't immediately justify or cut your pricing. Instead, recognize their worry and move the focus to value. A confident reaction could be:

"I absolutely understand that price is crucial. My objective isn't just to give you a haircut, it's to ensure you leave feeling more confident and looking your absolute best. Plus, I provide a monthly pre-booking discount that not only saves you money but also ensures your desired appointment time. That way, you're guaranteed a fresh cut without the stress of scheduling last-minute."

Similarly, long wait periods can be annoying for clients. If a client complains, "The wait is too long," don't brush it off. Instead, turn it into a chance to enhance their experience:

"I want to respect your time, and I appreciate your patience. Let's set you up with a standing appointment, so you'll always have an assured space. Plus, for pre-booking, you'll get priority scheduling, meaning no more long waits."

And then, there's the fear of losing a devoted client. If someone remarks, "I've been thinking of trying a new barber," don't take offense or act defensive. Instead, reaffirm their significance to you:

"I get it, trying new things is part of life! But before you decide, let me make sure your next cut is right for you. If there's anything I can improve or alter, let me know. Your satisfaction is my main priority, and I want to ensure you always leave my chair feeling like your best self."

A wealth-building barber doesn't fear objections instead he welcomes them as possibilities to develop client trust. Clients don't always need a reduced price; what they genuinely seek is more perceived value. When you take the time to address issues with confidence and comfort, you raise your service beyond merely a transaction. You're not just a barber, you're a trusted expert, a professional who knows the significance of customer relationships. By mastering the art of managing objections, you turn hesitations into loyalty and loyalty into long-term prosperity.

Retaining Clients Through an Unmatched Experience

Loyalty isn't built at the register, it's built in the experience.

The three main reasons clients keep coming back:

1. They trust your professionalism.
2. They love the quality of your service.
3. They enjoy the shop environment & conversations.

Client Retention Strategies for Barbers

- Personalized Service: Keep track of their chosen styles, hair concerns, and even life events. A simple question, "How was your daughter's graduation?" fosters emotional commitment.

- Prepaid monthly memberships, referral discounts, or unique VIP treatment for frequent clients are all examples of loyalty incentives.

- Engaging Shop Environment: Your shop should be clean and welcoming, making every customer feel like they belong.

- Consistency: The best cut you provide should be the same every time.

A client books biweekly but then stops coming. Instead of waiting, send a brief follow-up text like this: "*Hey Sam, I haven't seen you in a while, just wanted to check in and see how you're doing." I hope all is okay! Let me know when you're ready for your next haircut."* Small gestures lead to long-term wealth. Your clients are more than simply consumers; they are your business partners in success.

John's Journey: From Cuts to Contracts

John had refined his craft behind the chair, offering sharp fades and precise cuts that drew clients back. But something was missing: financial stability outside the barbershop. While his chair was constantly full, his bank account did not reflect the prosperity he desired. He realized that retention was more than just keeping customers in his store; it was also about leveraging that loyalty into long-term financial success.

Rather than seeing each client as just another cut, John established genuine relationships. He knew his clients' names, family history, and even their financial aspirations. One day, a long-time client said that he was having trouble finding a nice rental home. That's when John had an epiphany: he could own the properties his clients rented. Within a few years, he had converted his gains into assets, purchasing rental houses that his clients lived in. His barbershop became more than just a grooming hub; it also served as the cornerstone of his fortune.

John generated numerous income streams by leveraging client retention into real estate. His clients were paying him not only for haircuts but also for rent. He'd turned his barbershop relationships into long-term financial security.

The Final Thought

Client retention is more than just keeping your books full; it is about cultivating connections that lead to long-term financial security. Every client that enters through your door is an opportunity to develop a long-term consumer base. You may differentiate yourself from the competition by continuously providing a high-quality experience, proactively addressing issues, and making each visit an event worth returning for.

Remember that a great wealth-building barber is not the one with the most clients now, but the one whose clients will still be there 10 years from now.

Summary of Key Takeaways

- Client retention is the cornerstone of wealth creation and bear it in mind that long-term clients offer consistent, recurrent income that feeds investments.

- People buy experience, trust, and connections, not just haircuts. How you treat clients influences how much they appreciate your services.

- Anticipate and meet your client's demands. Whether it's grooming guidance, financial education, or real estate solutions, being the go-to source fosters more loyalty.

- John's path tells us that wealth creation requires working smarter rather than harder.

- Each client represents an opportunity. Strong relationships, whether through referrals, real estate, or commercial endeavors, lead to new income opportunities.

Mastering client retention is more than just developing a book of business; it's also about constructing a financial future. Your clients are more than just appointments; they are the key to unlocking your full earning potential. Begin treating them as long-term partners in your success!

Revision Questions

1. What makes your most loyal clients stick with you? Identify three essential factors and devise strategies to enhance those traits in your service.

____

____

____

____

____

____

____

____

____

____

____

____

____

____

2. John converted his barbershop relationships into real estate money. What unique ways can you turn your client base into long-term cash opportunities?

____

____

____

____

____

____

____

____

____

____

____

____

____

____

3. Assume a high-paying client suddenly quits booking with you. What proactive measures would you take to reengage them and assure their return?

____

____

____

____

____

____

____

____

____

____

____

____

____

____

4. If you had an extra $10,000 today, how would you use it to improve client retention and business growth? Consider new services, loyalty programs, or store enhancements.

____

____

____

____

____

____

____

____

____

____

____

____

____

____

5. Social media is an effective retention technique. How might Instagram, TikTok, and YouTube help you deepen

your customer relationships and keep them interested in between visits?

____

____

____

____

____

____

____

____

____

____

____

____

____

____

6. How can you add value beyond haircuts? Consider partnerships, membership programs, or special services tailored to your clients' lives.

CHAPTER 9

The Barber's Blueprint for Business Growth

"You're not just cutting hair; you're cutting a path to financial freedom. The barbershop is your foundation, but your vision determines how far you go." – Unknown

Success in the barbering industry is more than just cutting hair; it is about creating a business, a brand, and a financial basis that will secure long-term wealth. The capacity to grow as a barber is inextricably related to the ability to form connections, understand what clients genuinely want, and develop plans for long-term financial success. Every barber wishes to increase their earnings, but only a few realize that the key to getting more money is not working more, but working smarter.

Understanding What Clients Truly Want

Many barbers believe that personal successes, such as upgrading to premium tools, mastering the current trends, or obtaining more social media followers, are the key to success. However, while these factors can help a barber's image, they cannot guarantee client retention. Clients are more concerned with how you make them feel than with the trophies on your wall or the type of clippers you use.

When a client arrives at your shop, they want more than simply a haircut. They want confidence, convenience, and a service that matches their lifestyle. To create a great business, barbers must understand that every client asks themselves the following questions:

- **"What's in it for me?"**
- **"Will this barber make me look and feel better?"**
- **"Is my time being valued?"**
- **"Am I getting a return on my investment?"**

Clients do not buy features, they buy advantages. While a strong Instagram presence may initially draw them in, it is the regular delivery of content that keeps them coming back. Understanding what genuinely matters to clients enables barbers to present themselves as vital, resulting in business based on loyalty rather than one-time transactions.

Building a Strong Brand That Works for You

A strong brand is more than just a name and a logo, it is the reputation that precedes you. When your brand is well-known, people will refer you to their friends and family before ever sitting in your chair. It creates an identity that sets you apart from every other barber on the market. Instead of always hunting for new clients, your existing ones will keep coming back because they associate your name with stability, professionalism, and quality.

One of the major advantages of having a clearly defined brand is that it increases your perceived value. When customers identify your brand with exceptional service, their focus shifts from price to experience. They no longer see haircuts as an expense but as an investment in their own confidence and image. When the value is obvious, pricing issues vanish. Clients will no longer ask, *"How much do you charge?"* since they understand that the service you provide is worth every penny.

Beyond the financial benefits, a great brand promotes loyalty and emotional connection. When clients feel linked to your firm, they are more likely to remain loyal, pay higher prices, and become advocates who actively refer others to you. This creates a feedback loop in which your reputation continues to benefit you, attracting high-quality clients without requiring continuous marketing efforts.

What Are You Actually Selling?

Ask any barber what they sell, and the majority will say *"a haircut."* Some could say *"My time."* While these responses appear rational, they fail to represent the true value that clients want. Clients come for more than simply a haircut; they want the experience. A simple service transaction may bring them in the door, but a premium grooming experience is what keeps them returning and eager to pay more.

Instead of viewing your business as simply cutting hair, evaluate what you actually provide:

- **Confidence** - Every client wants to leave your shop feeling like the greatest version of themselves. A fantastic haircut can promote self-esteem, help individuals create a good first impression, and improve both their personal and professional lives.

- **Efficiency** - Time is valuable. Clients value a smooth and hassle-free experience, from easy booking to efficient service that fits their schedule.

- **A barber** - Client connection is based on trust. Clients return to barbers who understand their needs and make them feel at ease in the chair.

- **Luxury** - Offering a premium experience helps customers feel unique. When you establish an environment in which customers feel valued, they will be willing to pay more for your services.

When you change your perspective from selling a simple service to providing an experience, you rise above the competition. The idea is to produce something memorable, like an experience so pleasurable that clients will not contemplate going anyplace else.

The Secret to Earning More Without Working Harder

One of the most common mistakes barbers make is attempting to raise prices without boosting their value. Clients will not pay more simply because you want them to. If you want to earn more, you must offer more.

Jim Rohn once famously stated, *"We don't get paid for the hour; we get paid for the value we bring to the hour."* This principle is perfectly applicable to the barbershop industry. Your income is directly related to the value you deliver.

Here are some important techniques to boost your value:

- Upsell premium services: Offering scalp treatments, facial grooming, or hair replacement units can greatly increase your income per client. These services cost minimal additional time but provide significant benefits.

- Educate your clients. Teach clients about proper hair care, maintenance habits, and the finest products for their specific hair type. When you establish yourself as a trustworthy expert, people are more likely to purchase recommended products and services.

- Enhance the consumer experience -Make each visit feel unique. Provide hot towel treatments, complimentary refreshments, or loyalty incentives to create a premium atmosphere.

- Introduce membership or loyalty programs. Offer exclusive perks to returning customers, such as priority scheduling, discounted packages, or referral bonuses.

Barbers that prioritize value over volume can considerably enhance their revenue without working additional hours. The goal is not to cut more heads, but to make each client feel that their experience was worth every penny.

Maximizing Downtime to Grow Your Business

Every barber faces quiet periods throughout the week, but the most successful barbers make the most of their time. Instead of mindlessly scrolling through social media or watching Netflix, view downtime as an opportunity to expand and improve your business.

Here's how to use your free time productively:

- **Sharpen your skills:** Stay ahead of the competition by always refining your techniques. Watch seminars, participate in workshops, or practice new cutting techniques. Your value rises as your skill level increases.

- **Improve your marketing strategies:** Rather than simply perusing Instagram, produce intriguing material that highlights your expertise. To attract new clients, share transformation films, styling suggestions, or behind-the-scenes insights into your procedure.

- **Strengthen client relationships:** Use quiet hours to contact previous clients, send personalized appointment reminders, or follow up with those who haven't visited in a while. A brief message will bring them back to your seat.

- **Plan for growth:** Use your free time to plan future business plans. Are there any new services you could introduce? Should you invest in real estate? Could you start your own shop? Thinking ahead sets you up for long-term success.

Your downtime is *your preparation time*. Every minute you spend learning, strategizing, or developing your business will pay dividends in the long term. Instead of waiting for possibilities, use your time to create them.

John's Journey: From Barber to Business Mogul

John has always been a standout barber, recognized for his precise cuts and engaging personality. However, he realized that simply cutting hair was not the key to long-term prosperity; he needed to create a business that worked for him. He began by honing his brand, making every client encounter memorable and unique. Instead of viewing each haircut as a business, he prioritized making clients feel appreciated, heard, and ready to return.

John also understood the power of marketing. He used social media not only to promote his work, but also to share a tale about his journey, craft, and the transformations his clients underwent in his chair. He introduced loyalty programs, and personalized services, and grew his influence through networking with other local businesses.

Over time, John's fame spread beyond his shop. He started selling branded grooming items, hosting training sessions, and investing in real estate. His barbershop was more than simply a location to get haircuts; it was a brand, a community, and a legacy of financial independence. John's tale demonstrates that a barber is more than just someone who cuts hair; he is an entrepreneur, thinker, and money maker.

Final Thoughts

Success in our sector is not about working every day without a financial strategy; it is about developing mechanisms that allow money to work for you. Barbers can develop genuine wealth by focusing on customer relationships, branding, value-driven services, and profitable business tactics, rather than just making a living.

The question isn't simply "How many clients do I have?" nevertheless: "How many of my clients will be with me in five or ten years?" When you create a long-term vision, the game changes. Begin viewing every cut as an investment, every client as an opportunity, and every moment as a step toward financial independence. Wealth does not grow overnight, but with the appropriate mindset and planned action, any barber can transform their chair into a portal to long-term prosperity. Now is the time to think large, construct smarter, and invest for the future.

Summary of Key Takeaways

- Clients are the foundation of your wealth. Building strong relationships and retaining clients is key to financial stability.
- Branding matters. Your name, reputation, and consistency separate you from the competition.
- Marketing isn't just for big businesses. Strategic promotions, word-of-mouth referrals, and social media engagement elevate your business.
- A good barber sells more than haircuts. You're selling confidence, experience, and value that clients can't find elsewhere.
- Expand beyond the chair. Whether it's product sales, mentorship, or real estate investments, leverage your skills to create multiple income streams.

By embracing the mindset of a wealth-building barber, you can transform your career from a job into a thriving business empire. Your success isn't limited by the chair you stand behind, it's defined by the vision you have for your future.

Revision Questions

1. What specific branding methods can you use to position yourself as the go-to barber in your community?

____

____

____

____

____

____

____

____

____

____

____

____

____

____

2. How can you use client feedback to improve your services and keep more clients?

____

____

____

____

____

____

____

____

____

____

____

____

____

____

3. What would your loyalty program look like if you were in charge of developing it? How would it assist you and your clients?

____

____

____

____

____

____

____

____

____

____

____

____

____

____

4. What steps can you take today to begin diversifying your income beyond haircutting?

____

____

____

____

____

____

____

____

____

____

____

____

____

____

5. How can social media assist you not only attract clients but also in establishing yourself as a business owner rather than just a barber?

____

____

____

____

____

____

____

____

____

____

____

____

____

____

6. Assume you're giving business advice to a new barber. What's the most crucial lesson from this chapter that you'd share with them?

____

____

____

____

CONCLUDING CHAPTERS

Lessons Learned

Looking back, it's obvious that working smarter, not harder, is the key to financial freedom. A mental change is necessary to achieve financial independence, whether one chooses to accumulate cash or master the art of credit-based leverage. What matters most in order to accumulate and preserve riches? One must be financially literate. This goes beyond simple financial gain; it's about creating wealth that grows on its own, and that works for you. The leap from merely surviving to truly thriving is a matter of discipline, strategy, and the bravery to take measured risks.

Realizing that wealth is not made by a single action but by a series of consistent, deliberate choices over time is another critical lesson. Little decisions, like saving a little money, investing in your education, or taking a measured risk, add up to big changes. In spite of the fact that acquiring wealth takes time, the reward is always worth it.

Another important thing to remember is that you are an entrepreneur first and a barber second. A barbershop isn't only a chair and clippers like most of us believe it to be; it's the entryway to various income streams and legacy-building opportunities. Understanding cash flow, investing in assets, and utilizing credit responsibly are the skills that distinguish the 95% who struggle from the 1% who thrive.

Next Steps

Here's a roadmap for immediate, medium, and long-term actions to help you achieve financial success:

Immediate Actions:

1. Create a budget that represents your financial goals. Track your income and expenses weekly.

2. Open an investment account and start with that little and consistent contributions. Even $50 a week could potentially snowball into tremendous development over time.

3. Begin building your credit by assuring timely bill payments and minimizing your credit utilization.

4. Set up automatic transfers for savings and investments. Automating these little procedures removes the pressure of decision-making and assures continuous progress toward your financial goals.

5. Take advantage of free or low-cost educational materials, such as podcasts, books, or online courses, to increase your financial knowledge. Empowering yourself with information is a vital first step to developing sustainable wealth.

Medium-Term Actions:

1. Expand your revenue streams. Start selling grooming items or delivering premium services like consultations and specialized treatments.

2. Begin your first investing project. Whether it's a tiny piece of real estate or a diverse stock portfolio, start creating assets that provide cash flow.

3. Network with other professionals to learn advanced tactics and identify new prospects.

4. Consider joining a mastermind group of like-minded entrepreneurs. These groups can give you responsibility, fresh ideas, and critical contacts to help you achieve the next level.

5. Additionally, identify three areas in your organization where you may reduce unnecessary costs or enhance efficiency to maximize profitability. These tiny tweaks can have a large influence over time.

Long-Term Actions:

1. Diversify your investments further. Look into properties, businesses, and market opportunities to ensure your wealth isn't reliant on a single source.

2. Build a legacy plan. Establish trusts, retirement funds, and an estate plan to secure your family's future.

3. Mentor younger barbers or aspiring entrepreneurs. Sharing your knowledge not only strengthens your legacy but also uplifts the community.

4. Document your journey and lessons learned. Consider writing your own book or creating a course to share your experiences with a wider audience.

5. Think about succession planning. Who will take over your business when you step away? Ensuring a smooth transition is critical to maintaining the value and impact of what you've built.

Legacy Building

Barbers have a unique role in their communities, serving not just as service providers but as leaders and influencers. Beyond personal wealth-building, you have the opportunity to make a lasting impact:

- **Community Upliftment:** Use your success to sponsor local events, youth programs, or charity initiatives.

- **Mentorship:** Create programs that teach younger barbers about financial literacy and entrepreneurship.

- **Job Creation:** Expand your business to provide more employment opportunities in your community.

- **Generational Wealth:** Share your knowledge with family members to ensure the wealth-building mindset extends beyond your lifetime.

Imagine being remembered not simply for the quality of your fades, but for the lives you changed. When you invest in your community and mentor others, you have a long-lasting impact.

Beyond that, think about creating scholarships or funding programs for prospective barbers. Such activities not only broaden your effect but also strengthen your reputation as a community leader.

When you incorporate these activities into your journey, your success becomes more than just financial; it becomes transformative.

Reflection on John's Journey

Throughout the book, you've watched John's transition from a stressed-out barber juggling bills to a successful entrepreneur who understands cash flow, credit, and investment. His story shows that anyone can rise above the drudgery and achieve something greater. John did more than change his life; he left a legacy that will inspire others for years to come. You, like John, have the tools, methods, and mindset to overcome challenges and live a fulfilling life.

John's story not only demonstrates success but also provides a road map. From learning the value of discipline to utilizing credit wisely, his journey exemplifies the potential in all of us. By taking methodical actions and refusing to compromise, John transformed his barbershop into a center of opportunity, laying the groundwork for a future that would outlast him.

Final Thoughts

The journey doesn't finish here; it's merely the beginning. The lessons acquired and actions done today will shape not just your future but the futures of everyone you touch along the road. Remember, success isn't just about earning wealth—it's about using it to leave a mark that matters. Take these ideas, use them with purpose, and witness how your life and the lives of others are transformed.

Success isn't linear, and there will be setbacks. Embrace them as opportunities to learn and improve. Your legacy is established not just on your victories but on how you respond to challenges. The real question isn't whether you'll succeed, it's how enormous your effect will be.

Supplementary Sections

Financial Goals Tracker

Use this checklist to ensure you're staying on track with your financial goals:

Weekly Budget Tracking

Income: _________________________

Expenses: _________________________

Savings/Investments: _________________________

Credit Goals

Current Credit Score: _________________________

Target Credit Score: _________________________

Steps to Improve:

- On-time payments

- Lower utilization

- Dispute inaccuracies

Investment Milestones

Current Portfolio Value: ________________________

Target Portfolio Value: ________________________

Contributions per Month: ________________________

GLOSSARY

- **ARV (After Repair Value):** The estimated value of a property after renovations or enhancements.
- **Compound Interest:** Interest is calculated based on the initial principal and the accumulated interest of prior periods.
- **Cash Flow:** The net amount of cash being transported into and out of a business, demonstrating its ability to sustain operations and build wealth.
- **Equity:** The value of ownership of an asset, such as a property or business, after deducting obligations.
- **Leverage:** The use of borrowed funds or credit to increase the potential return on investment.
- **The margin of Safety:** The gap between the intrinsic worth of an investment and its market price, providing a buffer against losses.

- **Passive Income:** Earnings obtained with minimal active effort, frequently through investments, real estate, or royalties.

- **ROI (Return on Investment):** A measure used to evaluate the efficiency of an investment by comparing the return to its cost.

- **S&P 500:** A stock market index that tracks the performance of 500 of the largest publicly traded firms in the United States.

- **Asset Allocation:** The process of allocating investments among multiple asset categories, such as stocks, bonds, and real estate, to balance risk and reward.

- **Net Worth:** The entire value of all assets owned minus any obligations. This provides a glimpse of an individual's financial health.

- **Liquidity:** The ease with which an asset can be turned into cash without influencing its market value.

- **Dividend:** A percentage of a firm's earnings delivered to its shareholders as a reward for investing in the company.

- **Credit Utilization:** The percentage of available credit that a person uses. Lower utilization rates often enhance credit scores.

- **Depreciation:** The loss in the value of an asset over time, often due to wear and tear.

- **Index Fund:** A type of mutual fund designed to replicate the performance of a specific market index, such as the S&P 500.

Inflation: The rate at which the general level of prices for goods and services grows, diminishing the purchasing power of money over time.

www.ingramcontent.com/pod-product-compliance
Lightning Source LLC
LaVergne TN
LVHW062149200926
848484LV00007B/1886
9798989024513